THE GOSPEL FOR GEN Z

Jace Hunter

Copyright © by Jace Hunter 2024. All rights reserved.

Before this document is duplicated or reproduced in any manner, the publisher's consent must be gained. Therefore, the contents within can neither be stored electronically, transferred, nor kept in a database. Neither in Part nor full can the document be copied, scanned, faxed, or retained without approval from the publisher or creator.

Contents

The 'Gram Nativity

John the Baptist Gets the Party Started

The VIP's Public Debut

Devil Tries to Cancel Jesus

The First Followers

The Sick Get the Slick

Sermon on the Mount: The Blueprint

Jesus Feeds the 5K

Jesus Walks on Water

The Transfiguration: Jesus Glows Up

Jesus Heals a Blind Influencer

Lazarus: The Comeback King

The Last Supper: One Last Squad Pic

Betrayal for Clout

Jesus on Trial: The Cancel Culture

The Crucifixion: The Ultimate Sacrifice

The Resurrection: The Bounce Back

Road to Emmaus: The Unseen Follow

The Great Commission: The Send-Off

Peter Heals: Power Moves

Stephen: The First Martyr

Saul to Paul: The Ultimate Glow-Up

Peter's Vision: All Foods Fit

Paul's Missions: The OG Road Trips

The Shipwreck: Survival Mode

Love Is Lit

The Jailbreak Jam

The Philippian Vlogger

The Thessalonians Get a Group Chat

The Ephesians Get the Armor Drop

The Fruit of the Spirit Challenge

The Colossian Hype House

The Freedom Flex in Galatia

The Ultimate Influencer

The Faith Hall of Fame

The James Fit Check

The 1 Peter Pep Talk

The 2 Peter Warning Label

The 3 John Health Check

Jude's Throwback

The Revelation Reveal

The Seven Churches' DMs

The Heavenly Worship Sesh

The Dragon and the Comeback Kid

The Beast Mode Fail

The Angels' Hot Takes

The Babylon Block

The New 'Gram and the Real Influencer

TL; DR (TOO LONG; DIDN'T READ)

GLOSSARY

The 'Gram Nativity

Yo fam, so check it. There's this girl, Mary, just chilling, minding her own biz, when suddenly, an angel slides into her DMs and is like, "Hey girl, #Blessed, you're gonna have a baby!" And Mary's like, "Um, 'scuse me? No way, I'm not even married!" But the angel's like, "Nah, it's cool, it's God's baby. He's gonna be a legend."

So Mary's fiancé, Joseph, he's a solid dude, but he's hearing this and thinking, "This is some wild tea." But he gets his own angel visit, 'cause that's how God rolls, and the angel's like, "Bro, don't trip, it's all God's plan." So Joseph's down, 'cause he's ride or die like that.

Now, fast forward, and there's this census where everyone's gotta bounce back to their hometown to be counted. So Mary and Joseph hit the road to Bethlehem, and Mary's super preggers at this point. They roll up, but it's peak season, and every place is booked solid. They're outta luck, and Mary's about to pop, so they end up crashing in this rustic spot with animals and hay. Yeah, like a barn, 'cause no room in the inn, you feel?

Then it's go time, and Mary has the baby. They wrap Jesus up all snug, and they're like, "Well, guess a feeding trough's the crib for the night." Talk about a lowkey birth for the King of kings.

But get this, some shepherds are out in the fields, just doing their shepherd thing, and boom, an angelic flash mob lights up the sky. The shepherds are shook, but the angels are all singing and hyping up the birth of Jesus. They're like, "Yo, don't be scared, we've got the ultimate good news! The savior's born, and you'll find him in Bethlehem looking cozy in some swaddling clothes."

So the shepherds yeet over to Bethlehem, find baby Jesus, and they're mind-blown. They leave, telling everyone, and people are amazed at the 411 the shepherds are dropping.

Oh, and don't forget the wise guys, or magi, who scope out this new star and follow it, 'cause they know it's signaling something big. They roll up with the bougie gifts: gold, frankincense, and myrrh. Major clout for baby Jesus.

And that's how the original Christmas drop happened. Baby Jesus made His debut, and the 'gram—if it was a thing back then—would've been lit with the #Nativity vibes. Total influencer from day one. #BabyJesus #BlessedNativity #MangerScene #SaviorIsBorn 🌟⚫📕

John the Baptist Gets the Party Started

Aight, squad, let's spill the tea on John the Baptist, the og hype man for the Big J, that's Jesus if you ain't following.

John was this wild desert dude, living that minimalist life, rocking camel hair fits and snacking on locusts and wild honey. Total hipster vibes before it was cool. He was out there in the wilderness, vibing with nature, but also had a serious side hustle - he was all about that spiritual detox life.

So, he's by the river, getting his preach on, telling folks to hit that reset button on their lives with a lil' thing called baptism. "Repent, 'cause the kingdom is about to drop," he'd say. And peeps were listening, like his words were the latest track going viral.

John was all about that change-your-life challenge, calling peeps out to wash away the old and get ready for the new. And they were lining up, ready to dive into that river like it was the last drop of a limited sneaker release.

But John, he wasn't about that self-promo life. Nah, he was pointing to the upcoming main event, the one who would flip the script entirely. "I'm just the opening act," he'd say. "The headliner is about to take the stage, and trust, he's gonna bring the house down."

Then, plot twist, Jesus himself pulls up to the scene. John's like, "Fam, you're the VIP, why you need my river gig?" But Jesus is all about setting that example, so he gets baptized too, and the heavens go off with a wild approval rating. We're talking divine voice, doves – the full celestial package.

John's mission? To get the crowd hyped, the hearts prepped, and the stage set for Jesus to slide in and start that real revolution. It was the ultimate collab, and John was there to drop the mic (or, well, the staff) for what was about to be the sickest redemption tour ever.

So that's how JTB (John the Baptist, keep up) got the party started, paving the way with a baptismal pre-game for the history books. #BaptismChallenge #WildHoney #RepentAndRefresh #JohnTheBaptistHypeMan 🐪🍯🌊✨

The VIP's Public Debut

Yo, fam, let's dive into the ultimate drop—the public debut of the one and only VIP, Jesus, coming in hotter than a limited-edition sneaker on release day.

So here's the sitch: John the Baptist, the desert-dwelling influencer, just wrapped up his river rave with that baptismal splash. People are buzzing, hearts are woke, and the stage is set for the main event. Enter Jesus, fresh off his own baptism and ready to glow up.

Now, Jesus wasn't about to make his debut in some basic way. Nah, he went full beast mode and dipped out to the wilderness for a 40-day challenge against the ultimate troll, Satan. No food, no squad, just him and those wild temptation trials. But our guy J is unbothered, swatting away those evil pitches like a pro, 'cause he's got that divine connection.

Fast forward, and Jesus is ready to flex in public. He rolls up to Galilee, and it's like he's got that verified checkmark—people are taking notice. He's teaching in synagogues, and everyone's giving him the double-tap of approval. His rep is spreading like wildfire, and the follower count is just blowing up.

But what really gets the 'gram buzzing? Jesus hits up Capernaum, and it's like he dropped the hottest mixtape, but with miracles. Dude's healing folks left and right, casting out bad vibes (demons, yo), and he's got the whole place shook. People are like, "Who is this guy?"

And the miracles? They're like those viral clips that no one can stop sharing. A guy with an unclean spirit? Jesus is on it, telling that spirit to hit the road. Boom, the man's chilling, spirit-free. Peter's mother-in-law? Down with a fever, but Jesus is like, "Nah, girl, we got plans," and she's up and serving like nothing happened.

Word spreads so fast it's like everyone's on that fiber-optic internet. They're bringing all their sick to Jesus, and he's just dealing out health like it's Black Friday discounts. The hype is real, and it's clear—this

Jesus ain't just a one-hit-wonder; he's the full album and then some.

So that's the tea on Jesus' public debut. He wasn't just stepping onto the scene; he was setting it on fire, showing the world that the VIP had arrived, and this was just the beginning.

#JesusDebut   #MiracleDrop   #CapernaumCraze #DivineHypeMan 🔥🙌✨🌐

Devil Tries to Cancel Jesus

Aight, so peep this: After Jesus just absolutely crushed his baptism and was glowin' up all over Galilee, the devil tried to slide into the narrative tryna hit Jesus with that cancel culture.

So Jesus, being all about that grind, heads off to the desert for a major solo sesh—like, 40 days, no DoorDash, no Postmates, just him and the wild. That's when the ultimate clout-chaser, Satan, thinks he's got a prime opp to throw some shade.

First up, Satan sees Jesus is hangry after those 40 days and tries to get all sneaky like, "Yo, if you're really the Son of God, why don't you turn these stones to bread?" Like, as if hunger games could break our boy. But Jesus isn't about that easy life. He claps back with the Word, "Man shall not live on bread alone, but on every word that comes from the mouth of God." Talk about a mic drop moment.

Round two, Satan's getting desperate and takes Jesus to the highest point of the temple, throwing down a challenge like, "If you're God's son, just jump off, 'cause doesn't the scripture say you got angels on speed dial to catch you?" But Jesus ain't playing those games. He's like, "Nah, we're not supposed to test the Big G like that." Shut down again, Satan's 0 for 2.

Satan's pulling out all the stops now, taking Jesus to a mountain with some killer views and showing him all the kingdoms of the world. He's like, "All this clout can be yours if you hit that kneel button for me." But Jesus is all about that loyalty and integrity. He tells Satan to get lost, "Worship the Lord your God, and serve him only." And with that, Satan's cancel attempt is just cancelled.

Angels pull up to give Jesus the assist, 'cause he stood his ground like an absolute boss. So, Satan's little cancel culture plot? Yeah, that was a flop. Our guy J came out with more followers than ever, ready to start his ministry and change the game forever.

#JesusVsSatan   #TemptationFail

#CantCancelTheMessiah #DesertShowdown

The First Followers

Yo, let's spill the deets on how Jesus started building his day-one crew. This is like the origin story of the ultimate squad goals.

So Jesus is just vibing, walking by the Sea of Galilee, probably enjoying the breeze and the views, when he spots these two bros, Simon (who's also called Peter) and his bro Andrew. They're just tossing nets into the sea 'cause they're fishermen, right? That's their grind, their daily hustle.

But Jesus, he's about to flip their whole script. He strolls up to them and drops this epic one-liner: "Come, follow me, and I'll show you how to fish for people." Now, imagine that. Jesus is basically saying,

"Forget catching fish; I'm about to level up your life purpose."

And these guys? They don't even hesitate. They straight up drop their nets—it's like an instant follow-back. That's the kind of influence Jesus had.

Next thing, Jesus keeps it moving, walking further down the beach, and he peeps two other dudes, James and John, in the boat with their dad, Zebedee, fixing their nets. And Jesus must've had that charisma, 'cause he calls them out too.

What do they do? They hit that yeet button on their old life. They leave their pops with the family biz and take off after Jesus. They're not just looking for that clout; they're after something real, something deep.

So just like that, Jesus has got his core four. Peter, Andrew, James, John—these aren't just randoms; they're the first members of what's gonna be the most influential crew in history. They're the early adopters, the trendsetters, the ones who saw something in Jesus before he went viral.

And that's how Jesus began his journey, not solo, but with a squad that believed in the mission from the jump. They didn't need to see miracles or big speeches; they felt that realness and were ready to ride.

#FirstDisciples   #SquadUp   #FishersOfMen

#FollowMe 🐟👥🌊🚶✨

The Sick Get the Slick

Alright, let's scope out how Jesus was basically the G.O.A.T. of healers, making house calls cooler than any pop-up drop.

Word was out that Jesus wasn't just talking the talk; he was walking it out, too. So when he rolls through towns, peeps with all sorts of glitches—like being sick or rocked by some bad spirits—were lining up, hoping for that swipe-right from the man himself.

Now, Jesus wasn't about that selective VIP list; he was treating everyone's request like they had the blue check by their name. Got a fever? He's on it. Demons got you buggin'? He's got the block button for that. It was like He had the ultimate healing playlist, and everyone's tune was on it.

Take Peter's mother-in-law, for instance. She's laid up with a fever, and back then, that could be like, game over. But Jesus cruises in, takes her hand, and it's like he hit that reset button on her immune system. Next thing you know, she's up serving snacks like she just had a power nap instead of a health crisis.

And what's wild is Jesus wasn't just doing this for the clout. He'd heal someone and be like, "Keep it on the DL, yeah?" But you know how it is—someone gets that life glow-up, and they can't help but put it on blast. So his fame spread even faster, and the sick were getting the slick healing touch of Jesus.

The highlight reel doesn't stop there. Sunset hits, and everyone and their mom were showing up at the door with their sick. Who needs WebMD when you've got Jesus in town? He was healing them all, no appointment necessary, like some kind of divine doc.

But it wasn't just about the physical glow-up. Nah, Jesus was making sure their inside game was tight too. He was casting out the bad vibes and letting them know there's a new kind of life in town.

So yeah, the sick were getting the slick treatment from Jesus, showing everyone he's not just about the hype. He's the real deal, changing lives and setting the standard for what it means to care for your peeps.

#HealerOnDeck   #JesusSaves   #MiracleWave #HealthGlowUp 🚑✨🙏🔥

Sermon on the Mount: The Blueprint

Yo, fam, let's break down the most iconic TED Talk ever, but Jesus style—it's the Sermon on the Mount, and it's straight-up the blueprint for living your best life.

Jesus peeped the crowd building up, so he hiked up a hillside, took a seat, and his disciples rolled up to the front row. It was 'bout to get real—the Master Class was in session.

First off, Jesus starts spitting these blessings called the Beatitudes. It's like He's flipping the script on what it means to be blessed. It ain't about that bling or your follower count. Nah, He's talking 'bout the poor in spirit, those who mourn, the meek, peeps hungry for righteousness, the merciful, pure in heart, the peacemakers, and yeah, even those getting clapped back on for doing the right thing. Blessed are those who are real, raw, and making moves for good.

Then J-dawg moves on to the real talk about being salt and light. Like, stay savory, fam, and don't lose your flavor. Light up the world, don't hide that shine. You got a purpose to season and illuminate this world, so don't be sleepin' on your potential.

Jesus ain't done yet, though. He's laying down the law, but not like those old school rules. He's remixing it, taking those commandments and cranking 'em to 11. It ain't just about what you do; it's the vibe behind it—anger, lust, promises, revenge, love for your enemies, all that. He's calling peeps to a higher standard, like, love hard, stay humble, and be the real deal.

The sermon is straight fire, and He's just getting warmed up. Jesus talks about giving to the needy, but keep it lowkey—no need for that Insta story. Pray like you mean it, not just for the 'gram. And when you fast, don't make it a whole production. It's about that heart space, not the spotlight.

Then, Jesus drops this one-liner about treasures in heaven—stack those eternal investments where no one can snatch 'em. 'Cause where your treasure is, that's where you'll find your heart. And you can't serve two bosses, God and money. Pick a lane and ride hard.

The wisdom keeps flowing. Jesus is like, "Don't stress 'bout your life—what you'll eat, drink, or rock on your body." Life's more than the drip. Look at the birds and flowers, they're chilling, and they're fed and fitted by God. So if He's got them, He's got you.

Jesus wraps it up with the golden rule: "Do unto others as you'd have them do unto you." That's the mic drop. It's basic, but it's deep. That's the blueprint, the whole vibe check for life.

The sermon's a wrap, and the crowd's mind-blown. Jesus just laid out the master plan for life, and it's all about that heart transformation, that kingdom vibe. It's about being the kind of person that vibes so high, you're bringing a slice of heaven down to earth.

#SermonOnTheMount #Blessed #HigherVibes #HeartCheck #KingdomLiving 🔺🙌✨📜

Jesus Feeds the 5K

Yo, peeps, get this: Jesus pulled off the most epic foodie miracle that had everyone's Snapchat poppin'. We're talking the ultimate all-you-can-eat with just a starter pack. So here's the tea on how J fed the whole squad, and we ain't talking just a small group chat—this was a whole festival crowd, like 5K deep!

Jesus was out here healing and teaching, getting that influencer status 'cause his wisdom was straight fire. But as the day got its sunset glow, the disciples started getting all practical, like, "Yo, Jesus, this spot's remote af and it's getting late. Maybe hit pause and send the crowd to Chipotle or something?"

But Jesus, with that big energy, was like, "Nah, fam. You feed 'em." Disciples were shook. They're counting coins and thinking, "We got 5 loaves and 2 fish from this young blood in the crowd, but this is a snack, not a buffet."

Jesus just smiled, probably thinking #ChallengeAccepted. He tells the crowd to take a seat on the grass like they're at the chillest concert ever. He takes the five loaves and two fish, looks up to the heavens, and blesses it. Then he starts breaking bread like it's his mixtape, handing pieces to the disciples to distribute.

And fam, it's like the food just kept respawning. Everyone's eating, and it's not just a little nibble;

they're getting full. It's like that bottomless brunch vibe, but with bread and fish. We're talking about men, women, and kiddos all munching, and the mood is lit!

After everyone's had their fill, Jesus tells his crew to gather the leftovers, 'cause we ain't about wasting in this kingdom. They fill up 12 baskets with scraps. That's more leftovers than the original meal deal, and everyone's mind is blown!

So, what's the flex here? Jesus showed that when it looks like you're running on empty, with Him, you got more than enough. He turned a "might need to meal prep" sitch into a "we got leftovers for days" miracle.

This wasn't just about the grub; it was a whole visual of how Jesus provides and satisfies. He took the little they had and multiplied it to cover everyone and then some. Talk about the ultimate provider!

#JesusFeeds5K #MiracleMunchies #LoavesAndFishes #BlessedAndFed 🍞🐟🙏🎉

Jesus Walks on Water

Aight, fam, buckle up 'cause I'm 'bout to spill how Jesus totally slayed physics and had his squad's jaws hitting the floor.

So here's the sitch: The disciples were in this boat, right, just cruising across the lake 'cause Jesus told them to hit up the other side. Meanwhile, He's taking an "alone time" moment up on the hills, probably hitting that spiritual recharge with some prayer.

While Jesus is maxing and relaxing, the disciples are getting the opposite vibe. It's nighttime, and they're out there in the middle of Splash City, rowing against some mad waves and winds. We're talking serious "I didn't sign up for this" weather.

But then, in the creepiest part of night, Jesus decides it's time to catch up with his crew. And how does He roll up? My dude starts strutting on the water like it's fresh pavement. No boat, no surfboard, no floaties—just Him, walking like He's strolling in the park, but it's on the lake.

The disciples peep this figure doing the impossible, and they straight-up panic. They're thinking it's a ghost, 'cause what else could be strolling on H2O at 3 AM? They're scared out of their minds, screaming like they just saw the final boss in a horror game.

But Jesus, cool as ever, hits them with that "Chill, it's just me" vibe. "Take courage! It ain't no ghost. Don't be scurred," He says.

Now, Peter, he's got that mix of bravery and "hold my Red Bull" energy, and he's like, "Yo, Jesus, if that's really you, tell me to come out there on the water." You gotta hand it to Pete; he doesn't do boring.

Jesus just nods and says, "Bet, come through." So Peter hops out the boat and starts walking on water too! Homie is actually doing it, until he remembers he's in the middle of a wind cosplay and starts sinking 'cause of doubt.

He calls out, "Jesus, save me!" and Jesus does just that, grabbing his hand and being like, "Why you doubting, fam?"

They climb back into the boat, the wind cuts, and everyone's just mind-blown, worshiping Jesus, saying, "You're legit the Son of God."

And that's the story of how Jesus took a stroll on the lake, and showed once again that with faith, you can do the wildest things—even if that means defying gravity.

#JesusWalksOnWater #WaterStrider #FaithOverFear #MiracleMan 🚶‍♂️🌊🙌

The Transfiguration: Jesus Glows Up

Alright, tap in 'cause I'm 'bout to spill the celestial tea on Jesus' ultimate glow-up. This ain't your everyday makeover; we're talking a divine-level flex that had His squad absolutely shook.

So here's the scene: Jesus takes His inner circle—Peter, James, and John—up a high mountain to get away from the buzz. No one else around, just them and nature. But they weren't ready for the show they were 'bout to witness.

As they hit the peak, Jesus starts transforming right in front of their eyes. We're not talking a subtle glow; my man's face starts shining like the sun at high noon, and His clothes get so white and bright, even the best bleach couldn't compete. It's like He hit the ultra-high-def filter of holiness.

Then, outta nowhere, Moses and Elijah pop up in the chat, both long-time VIPs in the spiritual realm, and they start talking shop with Jesus. Moses and Elijah are kind of a big deal, representing the Law and the Prophets, and here they are, having a pow-wow with the main man.

Meanwhile, Peter's tripping over himself with excitement and blurts out, "Yo, Jesus, it's dope that we're here to see this! Let's set up three tents: one for you, one for Moses, and one for Elijah." Peter's trying to preserve the moment, maybe thinking 'bout that Insta story that would break the internet.

But while he's still talking, this bright cloud overshadows them, and a voice from the cloud—yeah, you heard that right, a voice from a cloud—booms out, "This is my Son, whom I love; with Him, I am well pleased. Listen to Him!"

The boys hit the ground, scared out of their wits. But Jesus, being the bro He is, touches them and goes, "Get up, don't be afraid." And when they peek, it's just Jesus there, back to His no-filter self.

As they're trekking down the mountain, Jesus hits them with the "don't tell anyone what you saw until the Son of Man has been raised from the dead" line.

You can bet they kept that Snap in the vault, pondering that "raised from the dead" teaser.

So that's the story of when Jesus went full-on glow mode, a transfiguration to show His true form. It was a preview of the kingdom glow, a little heaven on earth, and a confirmation that Jesus is the real deal, the chosen One, the bridge between the law, the prophets, and the new covenant.

#Transfiguration #JesusGlowsUp
#MountainTopExperience #DivineGlow 📷✨🙏

Jesus Heals a Blind Influencer

Yo fam, strap in 'cause I'm 'bout to drop the deets on how Jesus came through with that vision upgrade for a blind influencer.

Check it—there's this guy, right? Let's call him Bart. Bart's been blind since his "born" status update, and he's chillin' by the roadside doing his thing, probably droppin' wisdom or sharing his story in the OG podcast style—no visuals, all audio.

Now Bart's got this rep as an influencer in his own right. He's got the voice, the following, people come to him to hear what's up even though he can't see the scene. But he's been hearing the buzz about Jesus, this miracle worker who's been trending all over with his parables and healing skills.

One day, Jesus rolls into Bart's hometown, and the hype is real. The streets are packed, like when a new iPhone drops, and everyone's there for it. Bart senses the commotion and does a quick Q&A. "What's the hype?" he asks. "It's Jesus of Nazareth," they tell him.

Bart's inner lightbulb flicks on. He starts shouting like he's trying to get a celeb's attention at a red-carpet event. "Yo, Jesus, Son of David, have mercy on me!" he yells, using that title 'cause he knows Jesus ain't just your average Joe.

People try to shush him 'cause they're all about that decorum life, but Bart? He ain't about to let this blue check verification moment slip. He turns up the volume, "SON OF DAVID, HAVE MERCY ON ME!"

Jesus stops. The crowd goes silent. That's it; Bart's got his attention. Jesus calls him over. Now, picture this: Bart, throwing his cloak aside, probably his most prized possession, and yeeting himself toward Jesus. That's commitment.

Jesus is all, "What do you want me to do for you?" As if He doesn't know. But that's Jesus, always letting you hit send on your own requests.

"Rabbi, I wanna see," Bart says. Straight to the point. No fluff.

Boom. Jesus is like, "Go, your faith has healed you." And just like that, Bart's vision goes from 404-not-found to full HD. He starts seeing everything—colors, faces, the sky, probably even noticing how dusty his sandals are for the first time.

And what does Bart do with his new sight? He doesn't just bounce. Nah, he follows Jesus down the road. Probably hitting that follow and subscribe, 'cause when you get that kind of life-changing glow-up, you stick with the source.

So that's the 411 on how Jesus healed a blind influencer. Goes to show, when you call out to Jesus with the realness and faith, He hears you. He's about flipping the script, turning your dark mode into perpetual brightness.

#JesusHeals   #BlindInfluencer   #FaithGlowUp #MiracleOnTheDaily 🙌👀💯

Lazarus: The Comeback King

Aight, y'all, get ready to double-tap the most epic comeback story ever. We're talkin' 'bout Lazarus, the dude who took "I woke up like this" to a whole new level.

So here's the tea: Lazarus, this well-known guy from Bethany, is super tight with Jesus. They're like the OG squad. But plot twist—Lazarus falls sick, like, "cancel all my plans" sick. His sisters, Mary and Martha, are buggin' out, so they slide into Jesus' DMs saying, "Lord, the one you love is sick."

Jesus, when he hears this, is all calm and says, "This sickness won't end in an L, but it's for the clout of God, so the Son of God can get those likes and shares through it." Basically, Jesus knew this was his chance to flex God's power big time.

But here's where it gets cray: Jesus doesn't rush. He chills for two more days, which has everyone trippin'. By the time he decides to yeet over to Bethany, Lazarus has already peaced out. Yep, he's dead-dead, been in the tomb for four days, and the whole 'hood is mourning.

Martha, upon hearing that Jesus is finally rolling up, meets him and is low-key salty. "Lord, if you had been here, my brother wouldn't have died," she says. But she still has that spark of faith, "Even now, I know that whatever you ask from God, God will give you."

Jesus hits her with, "Your brother will rise again." Martha's thinking endgame, resurrection at the last day, but Jesus is about to bring the plot twist of the century.

He declares, "I am the resurrection and the life." Drops the mic. Tells her straight up, anyone who believes in him will live, even if they die. And those living and believing in him will never really die. Then he asks her, "Do you believe this?"

Martha's all in, "Yes, Lord."

Now Mary pulls up, weeping, and the mourners are following her, probably expecting a funeral scene.

But Jesus is moved by all the feels and asks where Lazarus is laid.

They show him to the tomb, and Jesus is straight-up sobbing. Even God's Son feels the heavy stuff. He's not about that stone-cold life.

Jesus, in full boss mode, is like, "Roll the stone aside." But Martha's worried 'bout the stench 'cause it's been four days—Lazarus is practically a mummy by now.

Jesus is like, "Didn't I tell you that if you believe, you'd see the glory of God?" So they move the stone, and Jesus does a quick shoutout to his Dad upstairs, thanking Him for always listening.

Then, he yells, "Lazarus, come out!" No need for caps, 'cause when Jesus speaks, it's always in bold.

And would you believe it, Lazarus hits the ultimate "unmute." Dude comes out, wrapped up like a mummy, and Jesus is like, "Unwrap him and let him go."

So, Lazarus becomes the Comeback King, a living receipt of Jesus' power over death. And that's how Lazarus went from "RIP" to "BRB" in no time, all thanks to the Big J.

#LazarusComeback   #ResurrectionRealness
#DeathWhereIsYourVictory #JesusSaves 👑⚫⬛💯

The Last Supper: One Last Squad Pic

Yo, fam, you gotta hear about the most iconic squad pic in history, no cap. We're spilling the deets on The Last Supper, where Jesus and the disciples had one last fam dinner before things got 100.

It's just before the Passover and Jesus plans this low-key dinner with the twelve, his ride-or-dies. They find this upper room in the city and it's all set up for a major throwdown, the kind that makes you wanna update the 'Gram with the squad goals hashtag.

So they're all reclining at the table, Jesus and his closest peeps, and the vibes are bittersweet. Jesus knows this is his last chance to drop some wisdom before his big finale. He's got that "end of an era" look in his eyes.

He grabs the bread, gives props to the Big G (God, that is), and breaks it like he's sharing his last Oreo. "Take this and eat; this is my body," he says, passing it around. The crew is probably thinking this is some deep metaphor, but they roll with it.

Next up, he takes the cup, again giving thanks, and he's like, "Drink from it, all of you. This is my blood of the covenant, which is poured out for many for the forgiveness of sins." The disciples are sipping on this, probably confused, but they know Jesus is serving up something major.

Jesus is getting real, telling them things are about to get wild. He drops a bombshell that one of the squad is gonna betray him. Minds are blown, and it's all "Who is it, bro?" around the table. Judas plays it cool, but Jesus knows what's up, and it's no secret between them.

Then, Jesus starts talking legacy. He knows the clock's ticking and he's about to be trending on every platform for centuries to come. He talks about peace, love, and sticking together—real hallmark card stuff, but it hits different when it's your last night out.

The vibe gets heavy when Jesus starts talking about peacing out. The disciples are shook, not ready to lose their leader. But Jesus, he's the ultimate influencer, leaves them with some parting words about staying woke and changing the world.

Before they can even digest all this, Jesus hits them with one more twist. "One of y'all's gonna deny me, thrice." Peter's like, "Nah, fam, never." But Jesus knows the tea.

As dinner wraps up, they're all singing a hymn, probably feeling all the feels, and they head to the Mount of Olives. It's like the after-party nobody really wants to go to 'cause they know the night's about to get real.

So there you have it, The Last Supper wasn't just about the food. It was deep talks, real talk, and the last pic of the squad before Jesus had to bounce and do what he came to do. A meal that's been meme'd, painted, and preached about more than any other in history.

#LastSupper   #SquadGoals   #JesusFinalPost #OneLastPic 🍞🍷👥✨

Betrayal for Clout

Aight, listen up, 'cause this story's 'bout to get messy. We're talkin' 'bout the ultimate backstab for some clout: Judas and his 30 pieces of silver vibe check that went down in history.

So here's the sitch: Judas Iscariot, one of Jesus' OG crew, is feeling some type of way. Maybe he's lookin' for that influencer lifestyle, maybe he's just salty 'cause things aren't going as he planned. Either way, dude's got his eye on a payout and he's ready to trade his loyalty for some silver.

He slides into the Pharisees' DMs, those high-key clergymen who've been throwin' shade at Jesus for a minute. Judas is like, "Yo, what's it worth to ya if I serve Jesus up on a silver platter?" And they're all about that life, flashing the cash—30 pieces of silver to be exact.

No cap, Judas takes the deal. That's like hitting the follow button on the betrayal account. He's now got a side hustle that's about to go viral for all the wrong reasons.

Fast forward to the squad hangin' at the Last Supper, and Jesus is already hip to the whole thing. He's not throwing shade, but he's calling it out, "One of y'all is gonna betray me." The disciples are shook, throwing looks, asking, "I mean, it's not me, right?"

Jesus keeps it 100, dipping his bread with Judas and basically saying, "Go do what you gotta do." It's a mic drop moment 'cause Judas knows he's been seen. So, he bounces out to go get those coins, leaving behind his squad for a payday.

The plot twist comes at Gethsemane, that low-key garden where Jesus is praying, getting his mind right. Judas shows up with the clout chasers—guards armed to the teeth, sent by the chief priests. And how does Judas mark Jesus? With a kiss, fam. That's right, a kiss. Talk about a heart react gone wrong.

Jesus gets snatched up, and Judas? He's probably thinking he's just secured the bag. But that clout? It's a fast track to regret. Those 30 pieces of silver start feeling heavy, and not in the "my wallet's so full" way.

In the end, Judas can't even with himself. He tries to return the silver, but the Pharisees are like, "No refunds." That's when it hits him. He traded his squad, his morals, and his boy for some fleeting fame and a little bit of coin. Spoiler alert: it doesn't end well for him.

So, here's the moral of the story: chasing clout can lead to some serious downfall. Betrayal for a quick boost? It's never worth it. Keep it loyal, keep it real, and don't sell out your crew for a moment in the spotlight or some temporary gains.

#BetrayalForClout   #JudasNoJudas

#LoyaltyOverLikes #30PiecesOfRegret 💔⚫🚫🔥

Jesus on Trial: The Cancel Culture

Yo, the scene was set for the most iconic "cancel" attempt in history. We're talkin' 'bout Jesus of Nazareth, on trial in front of a jury that's thirstier for drama than followers on a clout-chaser's feed.

So Jesus, this carpenter-turned-viral-philosopher, has been stirring up the status quo, droppin' truth bombs and parables that have got everyone from the common folk to the blue checks talking. But not everyone's double-tapping his posts, you feel?

The religious elites, aka the Pharisees, are big mad. They've been the influencers of their day, but Jesus is out here threatening their engagement stats with his radical ideas of love and justice. So, they decide it's time to hit 'unfollow' in the most dramatic way possible.

They snatch Jesus up in the dead of night (talk about ghosting), and by morning, they've got him standing trial. But this isn't your usual courtroom drama; it's more like a Twitter mob ready to hit 'cancel' at the first slip-up.

Pilate, the Roman governor, is like the platform admin, tryna keep things from getting too toxic. He's got Jesus on the main stage, asking the crowd to drop a comment: what should he do with this man who's been out here changing lives and flipping tables (literally)?

The Pharisees are working the crowd, sliding into convos, and hyping up the hate. They want Jesus gone, deleted from the narrative 'cause he's bad for their brand. They're accusing him of all sorts of stuff, but Jesus? He's just standing there, not even clapping back. He's got that "seen it all before" vibe, and it's driving them wild.

Pilate's polling the audience, and the Pharisees have got the hashtag trending: #CrucifyHim. It's a full-blown cancel campaign, and Pilate's hands are tied by the RTs and likes.

But here's the kicker: Pilate knows Jesus hasn't actually broken any community guidelines. He's just out here being influential in ways that shake up the old guard. So, Pilate tries to hit 'mute' on the situation, offering to release Jesus as a Passover pardon.

The crowd ain't havin' it, though. They've been whipped into a frenzy by fake news and fear-mongering, and they want to see Jesus' account suspended, permanently. It's peak cancel culture, with the mob calling for a crucifixion.

In the end, Pilate caves, handing over the username and password to the crowd's demands. Jesus is sentenced to the ultimate block, all because he dared to spread a message that was too revolutionary for his haters to handle.

And that's how Jesus found himself up on that cross, his message of love pinned up for all to see, a retweet that would echo for millennia. The Pharisees thought they'd silenced a rival, but they didn't realize they were just setting up the biggest comeback story of all time.

The moral? Real influence ain't about the numbers or the noise; it's about staying true to your message, even when the world's tryna hit 'cancel.'

#JesusOnTrial   #CancelCultureCrucifixion
#PilatePardonFail   #EpicComebackLoading

■ 👤 🚫 ● 💯

The Crucifixion: The Ultimate Sacrifice

Brace yourselves, 'cause we're diving into the tale of the ultimate ghosting that turned into the most epic save-the-world story ever. We're talking 'bout the Crucifixion, fam, where Jesus took one for the team in the most legendary way possible.

So here's the deets: Jesus, the guy who's been blowing up everyone's feed with miracles and straight-up wisdom, is now in the middle of a hardcore betrayal saga. Judas, one of his day ones, just traded loyalty for some coin, and now Jesus is in the hands of the haters.

Fast forward to the main event: Jesus is up on that cross, and it's not for the 'likes.' He's surrounded by soldiers, thieves, and a crowd that's a mix of supporters dropping sad reacts and trolls just there for the drama.

Up there, Jesus is taking the L for humanity. It's the ultimate "it's not you, it's me" as he's literally suspended between heaven and earth, carrying the weight of every mess-up and bad choice ever made. Talk about being loaded with notifications.

The sky's going dark, and it's like the whole world's putting up the "Do Not Disturb" sign. Jesus shouts out, "It is finished," and that's no understatement. He's just hit 'send' on the biggest act of love known to mankind. Account suspended, but not for breaking the rules—nah, he's rewriting them.

People are watching, and the reactions are mixed. Some are crying, knowing this ain't right. Others are just there to see how it all goes down, not really getting the magnitude of this moment.

And then there's the earthquake—like, literal earth-shaking moment—as if the planet itself can't deal with what's just happened. Even the Roman centurion on duty's gotta admit, "Truly this was the Son of God." Talk about a verified account.

But hold up, this story doesn't end with a tombstone as the final post. This sacrifice? It's the set-up for the ultimate comeback—a resurrection that's gonna break the internet in three days flat. Jesus is about to show the world that even when you hit rock bottom, there's a way back up.

So, the Crucifixion? It wasn't just a tragic ending. It was Jesus going all-in for his peeps, carrying the block button for everyone else's mistakes so they could slide into God's DMs guilt-free.

That's the kind of love that doesn't just go viral—it changes lives, rewrites histories, and breaks the cycle of cancel culture for good.

#TheUltimateSacrifice   #CrucifixionChronicles #LoveWins #ComebackKing ■■💔👑■

The Resurrection: The Bounce Back

Yo, hold up! If you thought the timeline was wild before, peep this: Jesus just dropped the biggest plot twist in history. They thought they had Him on mute, but He's back on the feed with the ultimate bounce back—The Resurrection.

So, after that dark Friday when the haters thought they clapped Jesus' account for good, things were looking low-key bleak for the disciples. Their main man was gone, and it was like their whole world got hit with the blue screen of death.

But yo, Sunday's coming, and with it, the stone at Jesus' crypt was yeeted away like last year's memes. Mary Magdalene, real ride-or-die, rolls up to the tomb expecting the worst, but what does she find? That place is emptier than a ghosted chat—Jesus is MIA.

She's buggin', thinking someone's played the ultimate prank, when outta nowhere, Jesus hits her with the "Hey, it's me." Mary's shook. She can't believe it. This is no catfish; it's the real deal. Jesus is back online, and He's not just sliding into DMs; He's making appearances.

The disciples are low-key freaking out because their group chat's getting updates faster than they can refresh. Jesus is out here proving He's got the best connection, no server issues to speak of. He's popping up in locked rooms, on roads to Emmaus, even hosting beachside BBQs, serving up fish and wisdom.

This resurrection? It's like hitting the reset button on the whole game. Death got owned, and Jesus is handing out second chances like they're going viral. He's showing holes in His hands and side, not for clout, but to show He's legit, that love really does win.

But let's get real, it's not just about coming back from the dead. Jesus is laying down the ultimate flex: life's got ups and downs, but there's no L that can't be turned into a W. He's the blueprint for the biggest comeback of all time, showing everyone that the worst thing ain't the last thing.

For 40 days, Jesus is the main story, trending harder than any hashtag could capture. He's teaching, blessing, and prepping his crew for the next drop—the Holy Spirit, 'cause this story's to be continued.

When He finally peaces out, ascending to the cloud (and nah, not the data storage kind), He leaves the disciples with this hype: They're about to be influencers in their own right, spreading that good news to the ends of the earth.

The Resurrection? It's the ultimate bounce back. It's the reminder that no matter how hard the fail, there's always a chance to rise. Jesus didn't just beat the algorithm; He changed the whole platform.

#TheResurrection #EasterComeback

#DeathWhereIsYourVictory #HeIsRisenIndeed

■■💯■■■

Road to Emmaus: The Unseen Follow

Okay, fam, let's spill the tea on this biblical glow-up story known as the Road to Emmaus. Jesus just pulled off the most epic ghost-to-host move in history, and the disciples are still sleeping on it. But watch how Jesus flips the script and slides into a DM convo IRL on the down-low.

Here's the sitch: It's been three whole days since Jesus hit 'em with the "BRB" and then bounced back like He's the king of the weekend. Two of the squad, Cleopas and his homie, are hitting the road, trekking back to Emmaus, hearts low-key heavy 'cause their Messiah mixtape seemed to end on a sad track.

They're walking and talking, probs hitting up their stories with #SadReactOnly, when suddenly, this rando traveler pulls up. It's Jesus, but they're clueless—like when you don't recognize someone 'cause they switched up their profile pic.

Jesus plays it cool, all incognito, going, "Why the long faces, dudes?" They're like, "Bro, you must be the only one in Jerusalem not following the drama." And they spill the whole saga of how they thought Jesus was about to revolutionize their whole world, but then got shut down, and now there's chat that He's somehow back online?

Jesus listens to their vent sesh, nods, but then hits them with the real talk. He breaks it down, starting from Genesis and running through the prophets, showing them all the Easter eggs that pointed to this comeback story. He's giving them the ultimate thread, but they're still not putting two and two together.

They reach Emmaus, and the disciples are about to hit 'end chat' when Jesus acts like He's gonna keep on scrolling. But they're feeling the vibe and don't want the convo to drop, so they're like, "Yo, it's getting late, hit pause and stay with us."

So Jesus, He joins them at the table, and that's when the big reveal happens. He grabs the bread, blesses it, goes full beast mode and breaks it. Boom, just like that, their eyes are wide open, and they're like,

"OMG, it's Jesus!" But before they can even snap a pic, Jesus goes full ninja vanish on them.

The disciples are hyped. It's like they just had the ultimate follow back, and now everything's clicking. They're not just hearting the message; they're living it. They yeet back to Jerusalem ASAP to tell the Eleven that Jesus is no cap, the real MVP.

And that's the Road to Emmaus story, where Jesus shows that sometimes you gotta unfollow to get the follow back, and the truth might be walking with you, even when you're not clocking it.

#RoadToEmmaus #UnseenFollow #JesusIsSneaky #EyeOpener #BreadBrokeMindWoke

The Great Commission: The Send-Off

Aight, fam, it's time to spill on the most epic send-off in the Good Book. We're talking 'bout The Great Commission—when Jesus basically hit up His day ones with the ultimate group chat before He skydived into heaven. It's the final season finale where Jesus drops the mission and passes the torch to His followers.

So here's how it went down: Jesus has already broken the internet with His resurrection, right? He's been making appearances for forty days, going viral IRL with all kinds of mind-blowing content. The disciples are soaking it all up, but they're kinda curious 'bout what's next on the playlist.

They all squad up on this mountain, probably expecting some more miracle-type hype, but Jesus has got something else on deck. He's like, "Listen up, 'cause I'm about to drop the biggest collab invite ever."

Jesus starts with the flex to end all flexes: "All authority in heaven and on Earth's been handed to me," which is His way of saying He's the ultimate influencer, no blue check needed. Then He hits them with the real talk, "Go and make disciples of all the nations."

He's calling His crew to slide into the DMs of every culture, baptizing them into the fam and teaching them to live that good life He's been demoing. It's not just about hitting 'follow'; it's about transformation, leveling up the whole world.

But Jesus ain't leaving them on 'read.' He's like, "And yo, I'm with you 24/7, to the very end of the era." That's the heavenly hotspot—no dead zones, no dropped calls, just that eternal support.

The disciples are probably shook, 'cause this is the ultimate send-off. Jesus isn't just asking them to keep His story on their feed; He's handing over the account. They're the new content creators, set to spread the good news worldwide.

And with that, Jesus pulls the most legendary outro. He just ascends, leaving the disciples staring up like they're waiting for the 'Skip Ad' button to pop. But there's no ad coming—just the call to action. It's their turn to hit the 'share' button and go live with the message.

The Great Commission is where Jesus essentially says, "Tag, you're it!" to every one of His followers, passing the baton and trusting them to keep the legacy lit across continents and centuries. It's the divine challenge to keep the story trending and the community growing.

So, if you're feeling this, remember you're part of that chain. The send-off is still going strong, the mission's still live, and the support's eternal.

#TheGreatCommission #UltimateSendOff

#DiscipleSquad #GlobalChallenge #MissionLit

🔥 📱 🌐 ➡️ 🛂 🚀

Peter Heals: Power Moves

Yo, peeps, get ready to slide into one of the most lit stories of the early church where Peter, a straight-up apostle, is out here making power moves with some next-level healing vibes. We're talking about the time Peter was strutting through Jerusalem and straight-up flexed the power of faith.

Here's the deets: Peter's cruising by the temple, and there's this guy who's been lame from birth. My dude's been parked at the gate called Beautiful, clocking in every day, asking for those coins 'cause walking's a no-go for him. We're talking 0 steps on his health app, ever. Life's dealt him a tough hand, and he's just trying to make it through.

But then, Peter and John roll up, and this guy is doing his usual, "Spare some change?" routine. Except, Peter's got something better than silver or gold up his sleeve. He hits him with the eye contact and he's like, "Look at us." The guy's expecting a payday, but Peter's about to give him the glow-up of a lifetime.

Peter's all, "I ain't got that cash money, but what I do have, I'mma give to you." He reaches out, hits him with the name of Jesus Christ of Nazareth, and tells him to get those legs in the game. It's like he just dropped the hottest track and the beat's too fire for the guy to sit still.

And just like that, my guy's up! We're talking instant playlist update from lame to leaping. He's jumping around, throwing steps on the Fitbit like it's Black Friday. The crowd's going wild 'cause they've seen this dude at the Beautiful gate more times than they've seen ads on Insta. It's a legit miracle, and the temple's buzzing harder than a viral TikTok challenge.

Peter's not about taking the creds, though. He's redirecting all that hype to the big man upstairs. He tells the crowd this is all God's doing, through Jesus—the same one they were sleeping on and even had canceled just a while back. It's a total power move, showing that faith in Jesus has got more juice than any earthly clout.

This healing's not just a one-and-done for the 'gram; it's a sign that there's a new power player in town. Peter and the apostles are out here proving that Jesus left them stocked with the Holy Spirit, and they're not afraid to use it.

So the takeaway? Peter Heals: Power Moves edition is all about that faith flex. It's showing that with belief in the heart and Jesus as the plug, the lame can dance, the lost can be found, and the ordinary gets turned all the way up to extraordinary.

#PeterHeals #PowerMoves #FaithFlex #MiracleGlowUp #HolySpiritHype 🔥🙌💯🚀✨

Stephen: The First Martyr

Yo squad, gather 'round for the ultimate story of dedication and serious clout, 'cause we're diving into the saga of Stephen, the OG martyr. This dude was all about that faith life, and his exit was nothing short of legendary. We're talking major heart-eyes for the commitment, but also some real talk on how rough the early grind for the believers was.

Here's the 411: Stephen was one of the first deacons, straight-up chosen to help out with the daily drop of goods and services for the needy. But Stephen wasn't just your average help desk bro; he was stacked with grace and power, doing big things, wonders, and signs among the people. Like, if miracles were a

TikTok trend, Stephen was hitting the top of the For You page every time.

But not everyone was double-tapping on Stephen's posts. Some peeps from the Synagogue of the Freedmen started throwing shade, trying to cancel him 'cause they couldn't handle the truth bombs he was dropping about Jesus and the new way. They got salty, stirred up some drama, and even slid some fake news into the mix, saying Stephen was talking smack about Moses and God.

So, they drag Stephen in front of the council, and everyone's eyes are on him. But get this: Stephen's face is glowing like he's got the ring light of an angel on him—no cap. He's not sweating it; he's ready to spill the whole truth tea.

Homie launches into a full-on history lesson, from Abraham to Jesus, serving facts and calling out the big wigs for their betrayal and murder of the Righteous One. It's like he's hitting them with the read receipts of their ancestors' ghosting God's messengers.

But the council is on full tilt. They're grinding their teeth, all heated up. Stephen, though, he looks up, peepin' straight into heaven, and he's like, "Yo, I see the heavens open and the Son of Man standing on the right hand of God!" That's like claiming you just snapped a pic of the divine, and the council is having none of it.

They lose their minds, yeet him out of the city, and start chucking rocks at him. Stephen's on his knees, taking hits, but even then, he's got mad love for his attackers. Dude prays, "Lord, don't charge them with this sin," as he's signing off. And with that, he sleeps—like, the big sleep, the eternal log-off.

Stephen's story doesn't just trend for a day; it's the kind of commitment that echoes through history. He's the first one to go all in for his belief, paying the ultimate price for his faith in Jesus. Stephen set the bar high, reminding everyone that sometimes standing up for the truth can mean facing the ultimate downvote IRL.

So, when you're catching flak for keeping it real or standing up for what you believe in, just remember Stephen—the first martyr and the definition of "faith goals."

#StephenTheMartyr #OGFaithful #UltimateSacrifice #HistoryLesson #HeavenlyVisions 💯🪨⬛✨🙏

Saul to Paul: The Ultimate Glow-Up

Alright, fam, strap in 'cause we're about to unpack Saul's journey to becoming Paul, which is legit the most epic glow-up story of all time. This isn't your typical 10-year challenge or a before-and-after skincare routine; we're talking about a soul-level transformation that's got more fire than a viral dance challenge.

So here's the tea: Saul was this high-key Pharisee dude, the kind of guy who had all the laws memorized, like someone who knows all the cheat codes but plays the game on hardcore mode. He was zealous, which is ancient-speak for "super intense," and he had zero chill when it came to shutting down the early Christian squad.

The man was on a mission to cancel every follower of Jesus. Like, if hating on Christians was a sport, Saul was looking to be the GOAT. He even had official papers giving him the green light to drag any believer he found in Damascus back to Jerusalem for some serious consequences.

But hold up, 'cause here's where things get wild. Saul's en route to Damascus, probably planning his next big bust, when suddenly, a light from heaven hits him with the brightness of a million retweets. Dude falls to the ground, and then he hears this voice: "Saul, Saul, why you trolling me?"

It's Jesus, calling him out from the cloud, like, "Bro, every time you swipe at my followers, you swipe at me." Saul's shook. His eyes are open, but he can't see a thing. The original influencer himself has left Saul on read, and it's a major reality check.

So they lead Saul by the hand to Damascus, and for three days, he's blind and doesn't eat or drink anything. Talk about a detox. Meanwhile, Jesus hits up this disciple named Ananias in a DM and is like, "I've got a new assignment for you." Ananias is hesitant 'cause Saul's rep precedes him, but Jesus is all about that second chance life.

Ananias pulls up, lays hands on Saul, and it's like scales fall from Saul's eyes—literal and figurative. He gets baptized, and it's the start of his verified account as Paul. The man who was once the biggest hater of Christians is now about to slide into the apostle lineup and drop truth bombs across the Roman Empire.

Paul's glow-up is next-level. He's planting churches, writing part of the New Testament (the receipts of his faith journey), and turning the world upside down for Jesus. He goes from being the guy everyone in the Christian community left-swiped to the one they're all following.

This Saul to Paul saga is a straight-up reminder that nobody's beyond that life-changing glow-up. It doesn't matter if your past is more blemished than a bad skin day; there's always room for a plot twist. So whether you're looking for a fresh start or a total life makeover, take it from Paul—the ultimate glow-up could just be one blinding light away.

#SaultoPaul #GlowUpStory

#SoulLevelTransformation #SecondChances

#FaithJourney 🔥👀💧✨📖📕

Peter's Vision: All Foods Fit

Aight, foodies and followers, let's dish about the time Peter had the ultimate "all foods fit" moment. We're talking about a divine revelation that flipped the script on the munchies and opened the table for everyone. So, get ready to screenshot this spiritual snack because it's a game-changer.

Here's the sitch: Peter, that rockstar apostle, was chillin' on a rooftop in Joppa catching some Zs before lunch, probably dreaming of his next meal 'cause let's be real, who isn't? Suddenly, he's got this vision that's more vivid than an 8K TV. The heavens open up, and down comes this massive sheet tied up at the corners, looking like the world's biggest takeout bag straight from the sky.

But this isn't your regular delivery. It's packed with all kinds of four-footers, creepy-crawlers, and wing-flappers. We're talking animals that, according to the old-school law, were a big no-no for eating—like the ancient version of "Do Not Eat" labels.

Then, God's voice hits Peter's AirPods of the soul and is like, "Rise, Peter; kill and eat." But Peter, who's been keeping it Kosher since day one, is all, "No cap, Lord, I've never let anything impure or unclean hit my Insta-worthy plate."

God claps back, not once, not twice, but three times with the real talk: "Don't call anything impure that

God has made clean." By the time Peter's vision wraps and the sheet's yoinked back to heaven, he's got more questions than a viral tweet without context.

As Peter's noodling over this cosmic TikTok, some guys show up inviting him to Cornelius's house—a Gentile, aka non-Jew, who's also had an angelic cameo telling him to fetch Peter. The puzzle pieces click, and Peter's like, "Aha! This isn't just about food; it's about people!"

So, Peter dips out to Cornelius's pad, drops the mic with a sermon about Jesus, and the Holy Spirit shows up, showering everyone there with love and blessings, Jew and Gentile alike. The takeaway?

God's not about those dietary DMs anymore; He's flipped the script to "All Foods Fit." It's a clean plate policy, and everyone's invited to the table.

This divine dine-and-dash was God's way of saying the VIP section is closed. Faith in Jesus is the only membership card you need, and it's got unlimited plus-ones. So next time you're scrolling through your feed feeling like you don't belong, remember Peter's vision. The barriers are broken, the menu's open, and all are welcome to get served some grace.

#PetersVision #AllFoodsFit #HeavenlyTakeout #CleanPlateClub #FaithFeast 🍽️🙌🌐✨🕊️

Paul's Missions: The OG Road Trips

Yo, peeps! Buckle up 'cause we're about to roll out with the apostle Paul on his OG road trips. These aren't your run-of-the-mill vacays; we're talking miles on the sandals, spreading the good news like a viral trend. So let's hit the ancient GPS and track this epic influencer as he takes the message of Jesus cross-country.

Mission 1: The Starter Pack Tour

Paul, formerly known as Saul (peep the glow-up story above), hits the road with Barnabas. This dynamic duo is like the original travel vloggers, except they're dishing out hope and salvation instead of travel hacks. They're hopping from spot to spot, Antioch to

Cyprus, then over to southern Turkey—planting churches like they're dropping pins on Google Maps.

Mission 2: The Sequel That Slaps

After a quick intermission and a cast change (enter Silas), Paul's back at it again. This time he's got a dream that's basically a divine DM telling him to take his tour to Europe. They're cruising through Greece, flipping cities like Philippi, Thessalonica, and Corinth into hotspots of faith. It's all ship voyages, open-air forums, and even some jail time—'cause what's a road trip without a little drama?

Mission 3: The Trilogy Finale

Paul ain't done yet. He grabs his squad—Timothy and Titus are in the mix now—and they're off on the comeback tour. They hit Ephesus, where Paul's teaching game is so strong it causes a riot (talk about influence). He's writing letters left and right, like ancient texts that are part of the New Testament now. The man's a walking content creator, except instead of likes and shares, he's collecting souls.

The Side Quests

Let's not forget the side quests. Paul's not just a land traveler; this guy's got sea legs. Shipwrecks, snakebites, and getting stranded on islands (shoutout to Malta) are all part of the journey. He's also a tentmaker by trade, so he's about that hustle, showing that even apostles need a side gig.

The Legacy

Paul's missions are the stuff of legend. He's clocking in miles like nobody's business, spreading the gospel before it was cool. He's got this radical idea that whether you're Jew or Gentile, the love and grace of Jesus are for you—no exclusions.

And let's not forget the letters—Romans, Corinthians, Galatians, Ephesians, you name it. These aren't just postcards; they're life guides that have been hitting bestseller lists for centuries.

So when you're out there on your own road trips, remember the OG, Paul. He took the scenic route through trials, tribulations, and triumphs to share a message that's still retweeted in hearts and lives today.

#PaulsMissions #OGRoadTrips #ApostleAdventures

#GospelGrind #SpreadTheWord 🚶‍♂️💼⚪✨👑

The Shipwreck: Survival Mode

Listen up, fam, 'cause I'm about to spill the deets on the most intense episode of "I Shouldn't Be Alive" starring none other than the apostle Paul. This isn't your basic "lost at sea" Snapchat story; this is full-on survival mode with zero cell service. We're talking the ultimate shipwreck saga that'll have you thanking the 'Gram you're on dry land.

The Setup: Sailing the Struggle Bus

So Paul's cruising the Mediterranean on a wooden yeet yacht, heading to Rome 'cause he's got a court date with Caesar. Talk about influencer problems, right? But here's the twist: the ship's captain is ignoring all the weather warnings. They set sail into a nor'easter that's more savage than a Twitter cancel campaign.

The Storm: Wind's Got No Chill

This storm is throwing shade like it's got a personal beef with Paul. We're talking winds that are yeeting waves like they're trying to go viral. The crew's tossing cargo overboard like late-night regrets, but this tempest? She's not ghosting. For days, it's nothing but gray skies and big swells—major "doomscrolling" vibes.

The Realness: Angel Cameo

But hold up, an angel slides into Paul's DMs in the middle of the night with that divine reassurance: "Bruh, you'll make it to Rome, and all these squad members with you will be safe." Paul's got that peace in the chaos, a vibe check that says, "We got this."

Shipwrecked: Welcome to Island Life

Cut to: the ship's getting absolutely shredded by a sandbar—talk about a crash landing. The ship's falling apart like a poorly planned festival, but Paul's like, "Stay calm and float on." Everyone's grabbing planks and heading for the beach like it's a Black Friday sale.

The Island Beat: Malta Vibes

They all wash up on Malta, and the locals are serving up some serious hospitality. They start a bonfire, 'cause everyone's dripping and it's cold AF. Here's where it gets wild: Paul's gathering firewood, and a snake thinks it's a good idea to chomp on his hand. But our boy shakes it off into the fire like it's nothing. The islanders are waiting for him to drop dead, but Paul's just chilling. Instant legend status.

The Afterparty

While they're wintering on Malta, Paul's healing folks left and right, turning the island into a wellness retreat. By the time they're ready to sail again, he's basically the island MVP.

The Takeaway: Trust the Process

So what's the 411 from this shipwreck story? Even when life's got you in hardcore survival mode, there could be a message, a mission, or a miracle waiting in the wings. Paul showed us that whether you're riding first class or clinging to driftwood, keeping the faith can turn a disaster into a "How I Met an Angel" story.

And that's the tea on Paul's shipwreck. Next time you're in a tight spot, remember this OG survival mode moment. Keep your head up, your faith strong, and who knows? You might just come out the other side with a story to tell.

#TheShipwreck #SurvivalMode #ApostleAdventures #MaltaMVP #FaithOverFear ⛴️💔🌊🔥🐍✨

Love Is Lit 🔥

Yo, peeps! Let's chat about something that's straight fire: love. We're not just talking heart emojis and "u up?" texts. Nah, love is the real MVP, the glow-up we all crave. It's like the ultimate TikTok dance challenge everyone wants to nail. So, here's how love is keeping it 100 in the Gen Z universe.

Love Is Your Hype Squad 📣

Real talk, love isn't about flexing for the 'Gram or competing for clout. It's about finding your ride-or-die crew that hypes you up when you're low-key feeling yourself or when you're down bad. Love is when your squad has your back, gassing you up with every win and catching you on those Ls.

Love Is the Ultimate Collab 🖤

Think of love as the dopest collab track dropping on Spotify. It's about vibing together, creating that perfect harmony. You're sharing your playlists, mixing beats, and even when the rhythm changes, you're there, head-nodding to each other's life tunes.

Love Is Not Ghosting 💔🚫

Ghosting? Nah, that's the anti-love move. If love is lit, then ghosting is a busted lighter. Love keeps the convo going. It's double texts, FaceTime calls that last until 3 AM, and leaving voice notes that are like auditory hugs.

Love Is Doing the Most 🐻

When you're in love, you're all about doing the most. We're not just talking about extra AF birthday surprises or Valentine's Day on steroids. Love is doing the most in the everyday stuff. Picking up their fave bubble tea 'cause you know the day's been rough or sending memes just to snatch a smile.

Love Is Woke 💡

Love is woke, fam. It's about knowing what's up in the world and standing up for each other. It's being allies, advocating for what's right, and not just swiping past the tough stuff. Love educates, elevates, and activates.

Love Is Self-Care Sunday, Every Day 🛁

Self-love, y'all, it's where it's at. You can't be pouring from an empty cup. Love is treating yourself like you're the main character—'cause you are. It's face masks, it's journaling, it's doing you, for you.

Love Is Your Personal Brand 🖤

At the end of the day, love is what you're all about. It's in your bio, it's your vibe, it's your personal brand. It's being kind, genuine, and that positive influence that lights up your corner of the internet and IRL.

So, let's keep love lit. Let's make it the trend that never ends, the challenge that everyone nails, and the vibe that everyone wants to catch. 'Cause when love's in your feed, that's the content we all need.

#LoveIsLit   #RealTalk   #HypeSquad   #CollabLove

#WokeLove #SelfLoveEveryday 📱✨💯🔥

The Jailbreak Jam 🔔 🎶

Ayo, fam! Buckle up 'cause we're about to drop the beat on the most epic jailbreak story, and no cap, it's gonna be a banger. This ain't your average escape room gig; it's the apostle Paul and Silas in the clink, turning a tight situation into a straight-up concert. So let's get it and dive into The Jailbreak Jam.

The Setup: Catching Charges for Good Vibes Only

Paul and Silas were out there spreading good vibes and healing the masses when they caught some major shade. Some salty characters weren't vibing with their miracles, so they got our boys thrown into the slammer. Talk about a bad review, right?

The Lockup: Maximum Security Vibes

These two get tossed into the inner cell, like the VIP section of jail, but without any of the perks. We're talking shackles, guards, and a vibe so low it's practically underground. But here's where it gets lit: Paul and Silas didn't let that kill their mood.

The Playlist: Hymns on Blast

Instead of plotting an escape, they're like, "Yo, let's turn this cell into a studio." So they start dropping hymns and prayers like they're headlining Coachella. The acoustics are straight fire, and even the other prisoners are tuning in, 'cause who doesn't love a free concert?

The Earthquake: Bass Drop or Divine Intervention?

Just as their set's reaching peak fire, the earth hits them with the sickest bass drop. This quake is so hardcore it's shaking the foundations, popping doors off like they're nothing, and everyone's chains just fall off. If that's not divine DJing, I don't know what is.

The Plot Twist: Guard's Midnight Crisis

The guard wakes up, sees the doors wide open, and he's about to yeet himself out of sheer panic. But Paul's like, "Chill, dude. We're all here." The guard is shooketh to the core, thinking he's about to get fired into oblivion, but instead, he gets hit with the realness of their message.

The Afterparty: House Call and Baptism

So the guard's like, "You guys are the real deal," and takes them to his crib. He patches them up, gives them some grub, and then—plot twist—he and his whole household get baptized. It's like an afterparty with a side of salvation.

The Clout: Authorities Get Checked

Morning comes, and the authorities are trying to lowkey release Paul and Silas, hoping they'll just dip out quietly. But Paul pulls the citizen card and the authorities are tripping over themselves to apologize. Talk about a power move.

The Takeaway: Freedom Tracks

The Jailbreak Jam is the ultimate freedom track. It's about finding your rhythm even when you're cuffed, singing your heart out when the walls are closing in, and knowing that sometimes, the real shackles aren't the ones on your wrists.

Paul and Silas turned their lockdown into a sound-off, and that's the energy we need to channel. When life's got you behind bars, find your jam and who knows? You might just start an earthquake.

#TheJailbreakJam   #PaulAndSilas

#EarthquakeBassDrop   #FreedomTracks   #DivineDJ

🔔🎶✨🔒🙌

The Philippian Vlogger 🎬✨

Yo, squad! Get ready to hit that subscribe button 'cause we're diving into the life of the illest vlogger in Philippi. This isn't your average unboxing vid or a makeup tutorial. We're talking about Lydia, the og purple cloth mogul, and a total boss babe who turned her crib into the first crib-side church. Let's roll on this vlogger journey.

Unboxing the Blessings: Lydia's Luxe Life

Lydia was all about that hustle, dealing in that high-end purple fabric — you know, the kind that would make even the Kardashians double-tap. She was living that luxe life, but her spirit was on the hunt for something more legit than just racks and status.

Collabing with the Squad: Paul and Silas Feature

So this one day, she's by the river, probably thinking of her next vlog idea, when Paul and Silas drop in with the ultimate collab invite. They're talking about this guy Jesus, and it's not just some influencer gossip; it's the real tea. Lydia's heart vibes so hard with this that she decides to stan for life.

The Baptism Splash Challenge: Whole Crew Gets Wet

Lydia doesn't just slide into the fandom; she cannonballs into the baptism waters with her whole household. It's like the #SplashChallenge but with holy water, and suddenly her house is not just featuring purple cloth, but also the freshest faith on the block.

Hosting the Ultimate Meetup: Church Edition

Post-baptism, Lydia's like, "Let's turn my place into the hotspot for believers." She convinces Paul and Silas to kick it at her pad, and just like that, her home becomes the go-to spot for all the Philippi peeps looking for that spiritual glow-up.

The DIY Faith Decor: From Home to Haven

Lydia probably had the aesthetics on point, turning her home into a sanctuary that was both Instagrammable and inspirational. She was setting the scene for the first home-church, where breaking bread and sharing stories was the daily vlog content.

The Comment Section: Lydia's Impact

Lydia didn't just flex her faith; she opened up the comment section for dialogue and community. Her crib became the space where peeps could ask the real questions and find support among the followers. She was like the spiritual influencer encouraging everyone to hit like on God's grace.

The Subscriber Count: Growing the Follower Fam

Thanks to Lydia's vlogger vibes, the follower count in Philippi was on the rise. Her home welcomed all — no sub count too low, no troll too trollish. It was the start of something epic, with her baptism vlog probably hitting record views in heaven.

The Takeaway: Vlog Your Faith Journey

Lydia's story is all about vlogging your journey with authenticity. She showed us that when you find something real, you share it, you live it, and you create a space for others to join in. It's not about flexing for the 'Gram; it's about connecting IRL and making waves in your community.

So, Philippians, keep your notifications on for the next chapter of the faith journey because The Philippian Vlogger is just getting started, and this heavenly content is too good not to share.

#ThePhilippianVlogger #LydiaLuxeLife
#BaptismSplashChallenge #FaithInfluencer
#CommunityContent 📷✨👗🙏♥️

The Thessalonians Get a Group Chat

💬🔥

Yo, fam, let's spill the tea on how the Thessalonians took communication to the next level — they started a legit group chat, and it's not just for memes and making plans. It's about keeping that faith flame lit 24/7. So grab your phone, 'cause we're about to slide into the DMs of ancient times.

The Invite Drop: Joining Apostle Paul's VIP Chat

Apostle Paul, the ultimate influencer, decided to slide into the Thessalonians' DMs with some divine wisdom. He couldn't double-tap their stories or leave fire emojis on their posts, so he hit 'em up with some letters — think ancient WhatsApp broadcasts, but with scrolls instead of scrolls.

Notifications On: The Encouragement Ping

The Thessalonians' group chat was popping with all the good vibes. Paul was hitting them with daily drops of encouragement, reminding them to keep the faith on lock even when the Wi-Fi — I mean, the spirit — feels weak. It's like getting a "You got this!" text right when you need it.

The Meme Ministry: Spreading Joy with Scrolls

Imagine the memes if they had them. Every scroll was like a wholesome meme, spreading joy and keeping the squad tight. It was about lifting each other up with the textual equivalent of a high-five or a fist bump.

Read Receipts: Accountability Central

This group chat wasn't just for lurking; read receipts were always on. The Thessalonians were keeping each other in check, making sure everyone stayed woke in their faith and didn't sleep on God's messages. It's all about that spiritual accountability.

The Block Button: Avoiding Toxic Scrolls

Paul's messages were clear: block out the toxic noise. Haters, false prophets, and drama kings and queens had no place in this chat. It was all about that wholesome content, keeping the main thing the main thing — love and faith, no trolls allowed.

The Hashtag Blessings: #ThessaloniansStrong

Hashtags weren't a thing, but if they were, #ThessaloniansStrong would be trending. Their group chat was a thread of blessings, prayers, and all the positive vibes. They were the blueprint for a spiritual support system.

The Chat Pin: Keeping the Vision Alive

The Thessalonians pinned that chat to the top of their list. Paul's words were like daily devotionals, reminders to stay lit for Jesus even when the going got tough. It was the ancient 'pin chat' feature, keeping the vision front and center.

The Takeaway: Slide Into Faith DMs

The Thessalonians' group chat teaches us to keep our faith circle tight and our messages uplifting. It's about creating a space where you can be real, get that divine read, and share the hope. So go ahead, start that group chat, drop those encouraging texts, and keep your squad spiritually synced up.

In the end, whether it's scrolls or screens, the message is clear: stay connected, keep the faith, and use every platform — even a group chat — to spread the love and keep the hope hotline blinging.

#ThessaloniansGroupChat #FaithDMs
#SpiritualSquadGoals #ApostlePaulGotBars
#StayWokeStayBlessed 💬🙌📖🔥

The Ephesians Get the Armor Drop

Aight, y'all, it's time for the ultimate unboxing video, but ain't nobody waiting on a sneaker drop—this is the full-on Armor Drop for the Ephesians, and it's straight-up divine. Apostle Paul is out here acting like the spiritual hypebeast, dropping the must-cop gear for the soul. So flex your faith, 'cause this armor is legendary.

The Belt of Truth: Fact-Check Your Fit

First up, we got the Belt of Truth. This ain't just any belt—it's that Gucci of godliness, that clout of credibility. Paul's saying, wrap this around your waist and keep those spiritual pants on, 'cause nobody's got time for fake news or devilish deceptions. We're keeping it 100, no cap.

The Breastplate of Righteousness: Heart Guard

Next, we're fitting up with the Breastplate of Righteousness. This is the LV of virtue, the Chanel of sanctity, guarding your heart against those low-key toxic vibes. Keep your core drip in check, 'cause righteousness is the real OG of flexing.

The Shoes of Peace: Step Up Your Sole Game

Slide into the Shoes of Peace, the Yeezys of tranquility. Paul's telling us to step out with intention, ready to sprint or stroll on the gospel track. These kicks are made for walking, and that's just what they'll do—one of these days these shoes are gonna peace-walk all over you.

The Shield of Faith: Block Those Fiery DMs

Equip that Shield of Faith, the Supreme of defense. When those flaming arrows of doubt and haterade get shot your way, you gotta be ready to swerve and protect. This shield isn't just for decoration; it's for deflecting all the negative energy. So keep that faith on lock, and watch those flames fizzle out.

The Helmet of Salvation: Mindset is Everything

Pop on the Helmet of Salvation, 'cause your thoughts need that protection. This is the headspace where you store all the good stuff—hope, grace, and the big-ticket reminder that you're saved and sound. It's like the AirPods Max of mental peace; tune into salvation and tune out the sin static.

The Sword of the Spirit: Your Divine Clapback

And finally, don't forget to arm yourself with the Sword of the Spirit, the Word of God. It's sharper than any two-edged hype knife, carving through the noise and letting you clap back with all the divine power. This is your spiritual katana, your heavenly lightsaber, slicing through the darkness with truth and precision.

The Girdle of Readiness: Keep Your Armor On Point

Wrap it up with the Girdle of Readiness, 'cause being prepped for spiritual warfare is a full-time job. This is the accessory that keeps all your other armor in place, so you're not caught slipping when the battle hits.

The Takeaway: Stay Suited Up, Fam

The Ephesians got the memo: this armor drop isn't seasonal; it's eternal. It's about staying suited up, 'cause life's gonna try to throw some wild PvP action your way, and you gotta be ready to stand firm. So rock that armor with confidence, keep your faith fit fresh, and remember: you're not just battling for likes and follows, you're on the frontline for your soul.

#ArmorDrop #SpiritualHypebeast
#EphesiansStaySuited #FaithFit #SoulSoldiers
🛡️✨👊

The Fruit of the Spirit Challenge

Hey, fam! We're dropping the hottest challenge to hit your feed since the Ice Bucket vibes cooled off. It's time to level up your spirit game and get in on The Fruit of the Spirit Challenge. Apostle Paul's got the deets in Galatians, and it's a whole vibe check for your soul. So, are you ready to flex that inner glow-up? Let's get it!

Love: Ultimate Flex ♥

First up, we're throwing down the love challenge. How many random acts of kindness can you rack up today? Whether it's sending that supportive DM or buying coffee for the person behind you in line, get creative! Spread that love like you're trying to go viral, but keep it genuine—no clout chasers allowed.

Joy: Keep the Hype Real 🖤

Next, we're chasing those joy gains. Find what makes you laugh till you can't even and share that joy. Whether it's a TikTok that's got you rolling or just dancing in the rain, let that joy be infectious. Tag your friends, challenge 'em to create their joy moment, and keep the serotonin levels lit.

Peace: Zen Mode On 🧘

Time to channel that inner peace. Meditation challenge, anyone? Show us your zen space, hit that mindfulness session, and share your calm. Throw a peace sign in your posts and stories as a shoutout to the tranquility you're bringing to the timeline.

Patience: The Waiting Game

Oh, we know this one's tough. Patience in a fast-scroll world? Yep. Your challenge is to not just wait, but wait well. Show us how you're embracing the slow moments, maybe even letting someone else go first, or not rage-quitting when your game lags. Patience is a flex, so show us that wait-worthiness.

Kindness: Random Acts GOAT

Kindness is key, so you're up to bat. Drop a vid of you doing something kind for another, no matter how small it seems. It could be uplifting someone with a compliment or helping out at home or in the community. Let's trend #KindnessGOAT and make it a movement.

Goodness: Spotlight on Virtue 🌟

Goodness is the challenge to be your best self. Post about someone you admire for their goodness and then act on it. Volunteer, donate, or simply be that positive voice in someone's day. Make goodness go viral by being the role model in your squad.

Faithfulness: Loyalty Hashtag 🏆

Show us your commitment game. Whether it's sticking by a friend or staying true to your goals, share that loyalty. Post about promises kept, trust maintained, or how you're staying faithful to your personal growth. Hashtag it out with #LoyaltyWin.

Gentleness: Soft Power 💪

Flex that gentle strength. It's all about that soft power, so share moments when you chose understanding over anger, or a gentle word over a shout. Gentleness isn't weak; it's the true show of strength. Show us how you keep it cool under pressure.

Self-Control: Reign it In Challenge 🎮

Last but not least, let's see that self-control in action. Maybe it's saying no to that extra slice of cake, keeping your screen time in check, or just keeping your cool in an argument. Share your wins with #ReignItIn and inspire others to do the same.

The Wrap-Up: Fruitful Living 🏅

This challenge ain't about the follows or the likes; it's about growing that character. So get in on The Fruit of the Spirit Challenge and let's see those posts flood the feed. Tag your friends, keep the chain going, and let's make living right the trendiest thing out there.

#FruitOfTheSpiritChallenge   #CharacterGrowth #VibesCheck #SoulFlex 🍇🔥🏅

The Colossian Hype House 🏠💥

Yo, fam! Let's talk about the ultimate spiritual squad goals—the Colossian Hype House. Apostle Paul was sending out those ancient texts (more like scrolls, but you get it), and he wasn't just preaching; he was building a crew that's all about that Christ-centered clout. So, let's break down how the Colossians turned their city into the hype house where faith meets fire.

The Founder: Apostle Paul, the Visionary 📕✨

Paul, aka the spiritual entrepreneur, was crafting DMs from a distance, 'cause sometimes you gotta influence from afar. He was dropping lines of wisdom that hit harder than the latest drop on a hypebeast store. Paul was building a brand of believers who were all in on the faith flex.

The Members: Colossian Crew, the Faithful Fam

The Colossians were the day ones, the OG crew, the ride-or-die disciples who were ready to rep the gospel like it was the freshest fit of the season. They were the ones liking, sharing, and commenting with amen on all the wisdom Paul was dishing out.

The Content: Spiritual Snippets and Divine Drips

What's a hype house without that fire content? The Colossians were living out those holy how-tos, turning Paul's advice into lifestyle vlogs. Imagine the 'fit checks but for armor of God, the DIY prayer corners, and the faith challenges going viral among the believers.

The Collabs: Unity in the Community

The Colossian Hype House wasn't about solo stardom; it was all about that collab culture. They were networking with fellow hype houses (think Ephesians, Philippians, you name it) to spread the gospel like it's a trending hashtag. No subtweeting or shade, just pure partnership in the faith fam.

The Mission: Spreading the Gospel, Not the Gossip

Paul's letters were clear—gossip and drama were canceled. The mission was to put the good news on blast, not the latest scandal. So the Colossians stayed sharing testimonials, not tea, and lifting each other up instead of throwing shade.

The Merch: Spiritual Swag and Holy Fits 🖤👕

If the Colossians had a merch line, it'd be all about those virtues: hoodies stamped with humility, caps crowned with kindness, and tees tagged with temperance. Every piece would be a conversation starter, a statement of faith you could rock walking down the street.

The Challenges: Keeping the Faith Fresh and Fun 🎉🛡️

This hype house knew how to keep the faith fresh. They'd be hosting challenges like the 'Love Thy Neighbor' TikTok dance-offs or the 'Scripture Verse

Memory' rap battles. Keeping the Word alive and kicking, making sure everyone's spiritual game stayed sharp.

The Drop: When Grace Goes Viral 🎆 📱

The ultimate drop wasn't a limited sneaker or an exclusive track—it was grace, and it was free for everyone. The Colossian Hype House was about that grace drop, making sure everyone knew that access to faith was unlimited and all-inclusive.

The Takeaway: Be Like the Colossian Hype House 🏠💯

So, what's the vibe? The Colossian Hype House is the blueprint for how we should be coming together—building each other up, staying focused on the mission, and keeping the faith in everything we do. Whether in person or online, we're all called to create that spiritual hype, turning our collective clout into a force for good.

#ColossianHypeHouse #FaithFam

#SpiritualSquadGoals #ApostlePaulTheInfluencer

#GraceGoesViral 🏠 💥 🙌

The Freedom Flex in Galatia 🦅 🔓

Yo, Galatians! It's time to get lit with that Freedom Flex. Apostle Paul's out here serving straight-up truth tea, spilling the deets on what real freedom looks like. No cap, it's all about breaking those chains with some divine swag. So, let's get into this freedom manifesto, Gen Z edition.

The Backstory: Legalism vs. Liberty 🗿 ⚖️

Galatia was caught up in that old-school scene, thinking they could earn their way to the VIP section of heaven with those ancient laws and customs. Paul slides into the convo like, "Hold up, let me put you on to something real." He's preaching that Jesus already paid the tab, so trying to keep up with those outdated rules is like rocking last season's trends—pointless.

The Real Deal: Justified by Faith, Not by Fit Checks 🙌🏾

Here's the drop: Your clout with God ain't about what you rock on the outside; it's about that faith fit on the inside. Paul's flexing hard on the message that believing in Jesus is what justifies you. It's like a follow from the Most High, and once you've got that, it's instant verification—no blue check needed.

The Freedom Flex: Living in the Spirit #NoRestrictions 🕊️✨

Now, with the freedom flex comes big responsibility. Paul's not saying to wild out and do whatever. It's about living in the Spirit, which means your actions are driven by love, peace, and all those good vibes.

It's walking into the room and radiating positivity like you own the place, 'cause spiritually, you kinda do.

The Squad Goals: Love Your Neighbor, No Trolls Allowed ♥⊘🌷

This freedom means we're all about that love life—no, not the dating app kind, the 'love your neighbor like your playlist' kind. It's treating others with respect, not dragging them online or being a troll. Keep the squad supportive, inclusive, and all about that lift-each-other-up mentality.

The No Flex Zone: Humility Is The New Hype ●♛

In the Freedom Flex, humility is where it's at. It's like being the main character without needing to always be the center of attention. Paul's letter is clear: Don't get caught in your own hype, 'cause self-conceit is a major buzzkill. Keep it 100 and stay grounded.

The Clout That Counts: Serving One Another 🫶🔥

Real talk, the clout that counts in the Freedom Flex is how you serve others. It's the reposts for a cause, the volunteer work that doesn't make your Story, and the helping hand with no receipts. That's the kind of influence that turns heads in Galatia and beyond.

The Fit Check: Fruits of the Spirit 💯🍇

If the Freedom Flex had a fit check, it's all about rocking those Fruits of the Spirit. Love, joy, peace, patience, kindness, goodness, faithfulness, gentleness, and self-control—these are the accessories that never go out of style. So, stay dripped in the Spirit, 'cause it's a look that always slays.

The Wrap-Up: Live Free, Stay Fly 🎤 ✌️

Galatians, the Freedom Flex is the ultimate life hack. It's not about fronting for the 'gram or chasing empty likes. It's about living in that true freedom, where your soul's got that eternal glow-up. So, flex your freedom, keep it real, and let the Spirit lead the way.

#FreedomFlex   #GalatiaGlowUp   #FaithFits

#SpiritualSwag   #FruitsOfTheSpirit   #RealClout

🦅 🔓 💯 ✨

The Ultimate Influencer 🌟 📱

Aight, peeps, let's spill the real tea on who's slaying the game as The Ultimate Influencer. Forget the 'gram gods and TikTok titans, we're talking about the O.G. of influence that's been trending since ancient times – Y'all ready for this? It's Jesus Christ, the carpenter's kid who flipped the script and went mega-viral with just 12 followers. Let's break it down, Gen Z style.

The Bio: Son of God, Miracle Maestro 🌙✨

Jesus dropped into the human scene with the most low-key launch ever—born in a stable, no paparazzi, no blue checks. But don't let that manger start fool you; this dude was heaven's A-lister from day one. His bio's got 'Son of God' and 'Miracle Maestro' 'cause turning water into the finest vino and calming storms is just how He rolls.

The Content: Parables & Beatitudes, No Clickbait Needed 📖🚫

JC wasn't about that clickbait life. He spoke in parables and dropped beatitudes that had peeps rethinking their whole existence. Blessed are the poor in spirit? That's the kind of soulful content that gets you thinking deeper than any deep-dive thread.

The Collabs: Disciples and Tax Collectors, Inclusivity on Point 👥⚫

Jesus was all about those epic collabs. He wasn't just rolling with the 'cool kids'; He brought in fishermen, tax collectors, and even those society had ghosted.

His squad was diverse AF, and He showed mad love to everyone, no matter their follower count.

The #NoFilter Lifestyle: Authenticity is the Key 🔑💯

Talk about living that #NoFilter life. Jesus kept it 100 all the time. Walking on water, feeding the 5K with a couple of fish and loaves—no flex, just miracles. He wasn't about the facade; He was serving straight-up authenticity, and that's the real influencer goal.

The Challenges: Love Thy Neighbor, The OG Viral Challenge 📵🏆

Before all those viral dance-offs, Jesus hit 'em with the 'Love Thy Neighbor' challenge. It went harder than any TikTok trend because it wasn't just for the 'likes'—it was about changing lives and hearts. Talk about a challenge with eternal rewards.

The Merch: Crosses and Fishes, Symbol Game Strong ✝︎🐟

The Ultimate Influencer had that symbol game on lock. Crosses and fishes weren't just aesthetic; they were (and still are) the merch that represents something bigger than any brand collab. It's the swag with a message that's lasted millennia.

The Mission: Salvation for the Squad, Eternal Vibes Only ✝︎🙏

Jesus wasn't just building a brand; He was on a mission for salvation. His influence wasn't about temporary clout but eternal vibes. He came through with a message of redemption and a love so epic it's still trending.

The Ultimate Follow: The Path to Eternal Life, No Subs Needed 👑❤️

Following Jesus is the ultimate follow-back. It's not about social creds; it's about that path to eternal life. He doesn't care if you're verified or have a micro-following; His 'follow' button is there for everyone, no subs needed.

So, when you're scrolling through feeds of fit pics and flexes, just remember the influencer game was forever changed by a man who turned the world upside down with nothing but a message of love and hope. That, fam, is The Ultimate Influencer.

#UltimateInfluencer   #JesusChrist   #OGVibes

#EternalInfluence   #LoveChallenge   #NoFilterFaith

✶ ▌ ♥ ■ ●

The Faith Hall of Fame 🙏 🌟

Yo fam, let's roll out the red carpet and snap some holy selfies at the illest venue of all time—The Faith Hall of Fame. This is where the legends of the Good Book get their hype for keeping it 💯 with the Almighty. No blue checks, just pure trust and vibes. Let's meet the squad that's been serving spiritual goals since day one.

Noah - The Arkitect 🛖 🐾

First up, we got Noah, the original conservationist and the king of the "just trust me" build. My guy got the ultimate DIY project, crafting an ark with no YouTube tutorial, just divine DMs. Noah's the O.G. of the faith influencers, keeping his chill while everyone else was sleepin' on the forecast.

Abraham - The OG Wanderluster 🏴 ★

Next is Abraham, the dude who left it all behind 'cause God was like, "I got you a surprise, but it's location TBA." This legend is all about that nomadic influencer life—no permanent address, just stars in the sky and a promise that his fam would be LITerally as countless as the stars.

Sarah - Queen of Patience 👑 ⧗

Can't forget about Sarah, the original influencer in the art of waiting. Homegirl had patience thicker than the iPhone's waitlist. She laughed when told she'd have a kid in her golden years, but she had the last laugh when Isaac rolled up.

Moses - The Freedom Fighter 💪🔥

Big up Moses, the ex-royal who became the G.O.A.T. of liberators. This bro split seas, delivered the divine law, and was all about freeing the squad. His influencer game was so strong, even the Red Sea gave him a follow.

David - The Giant Slayer ●👑

Now, make some noise for David, the shepherd boy turned king who was serving Goliath-sized clapbacks with just a slingshot. The kid who was vibing with sheep became the hero with heart, proving size of your faith > size of your enemies.

Esther - The Royal Game-Changer 👑✨

Shoutout to Esther, the beauty with brains who flipped the script in the palace. She risked it all to save her peeps, proving that true influence comes from taking a stand—even when your knees are shaking.

Daniel - The Lion's BFF

Let's not sleep on Daniel, the ultimate survivor who was literally chilling in a den of hangry lions. Homie was so tight with God that even the lions weren't trying to mess with him. That's what you call beast mode faith.

Mary - The Ultimate Believer

Mary, the mother of Jesus, was the influencer that all other influencers aspire to be. She was like, "Imma carry the Son of God, no biggie," and just went with it. Talk about trust levels being on a hundred thousand trillion.

Paul - The Comeback Kid 💼👊

Last but not least, Paul, formerly known as Saul, who had the sickest character development. From Christian hunter to epistle author, he went from zero to hero, penning some of the most fire content in the New Testament.

Wrap-Up 🎤🎉

And there you have it, the cloud of witnesses that's been flexing their faith since ancient times. These influencers didn't need tech or trends; they had miracles and messages. They're the OGs of that eternal clout, and their legacy is still popping off.

So when you're hitting that scroll, remember the Faith Hall of Fame. These legends set the bar for the ultimate follow-back, and they're proof that when it comes to influence, it's the size of your heart and faith that truly counts.

#FaithHallofFame #SpiritualOGs #BibleLegends #TrustTheProcess #EternalClout 🙏🌟📖

The James Fit Check 👓 👞

Yo fam, let's break down the drip 'cause James just stepped out with a fit that's straight fire! My guy's got the threads talkin' and the 'gram double-tappin'. Here's the 411 on that biblical boi's fit check, Gen Z style.

Headgear: Crown of Faithfulness 👑 ✨

Starting at the top, James rocks that Crown of Faithfulness like no other. It's not your typical snapback or beanie; this headpiece is all about that spiritual swag. It's like an aura of good vibes and loyalty that just doesn't quit.

Top: Robe of Righteousness 🧥 🙌

Peep the outerwear! James is draped in that Robe of Righteousness, cut from the divine cloth of doing right by others. It's not just a statement piece; it's a lifestyle. That robe says, "I walk the talk," and trust, it never goes out of style.

Bottoms: Trousers of Tenacity 🩳 🏃

Dude's trousers are tailored with Tenacity—perfect for those long days grindin' out good deeds and staying steady in the faith race. They've got that spiritual stretch, making sure he's ready for any trial or tribulation that tries to trip him up.

Kicks: Sneakers of Speedy Service 👟 👟

Check those heavenly kicks! The Sneakers of Speedy Service are laced up and ready to sprint into service at a moment's notice. They're the Yeezys of yeetin' yourself into helping others, complete with angelic air soles for that cloud-nine comfort.

Accessories: Belt of Truth 🗣️✖️

James ain't slackin' when it comes to accessories, either. He's got that Belt of Truth cinched tight, keeping his fit—and his convictions—firmly in place. It's like the ultimate lie detector but for his waist, making sure he's not just flexing for the 'gram.

Bling: Chain of Charity 💎👊

No fit is complete without some ice, and James' Chain of Charity is the bling that shines brighter than a VSCO filter. It's made up of links forged from every act of kindness, and man, does it glisten with that good karma glow.

Wrist Game: Watch of Wisdom ⬢ 🛡

On the wrist, James sports the Watch of Wisdom that keeps him on God's time. It ticks not with minutes but with moments to make wise moves and spread some sage advice. It's the Rolex of revelation, always timeless.

The Vibe: Aura of Authenticity ✨ 🔥

But let's be real, the ultimate accessory that James rocks is his Aura of Authenticity. It's that unmistakable glow of someone who's genuine through and through. No filters, no flex, just 100% unadulterated realness.

So there you have it, the James Fit Check. It's not just about the threads; it's the character beneath that makes the man. James keeps it so fresh and so clean with a fit that's not just seen but felt. He's out here proving that the best fits are the ones that reflect your inner drip.

Keep stylin' and profilin', James. Your faith fit is what we're all here for.

#JamesFitCheck   #FaithFashion   #GenZSlang #SpiritualSwag #BiblicalDrip 🕶️👟✨

The 1 Peter Pep Talk 🚀🔥

Aight, here it go, the spiritual hype session straight from ya boi, 1 Peter, servin' up that divine tea with a side of real talk. Time to get those spirits lifted and that motivation maxed out. Let's get it, Gen Z!

Yo squad, listen up! 🎧

Life's hitting hard rn, huh? Feels like we're stuck in some eternal loading screen with the spinning wheel of doom. But hold up, Peter's got that ancient wisdom to keep us going. 💭✨

Keep Ya Head Up:

First things first, you gotta keep that head up. No cap, you're chosen, royal, and straight-up holy. You've got that spiritual DNA that's all about shining light in the dark corners of your feed. 💡👑

Stay Litty:

Stay lit with that inner fire. The world's gonna throw shade, but you've got that eternal flame. Those trials? They're just the tea getting steeped, fam. It's all about brewing strength, resilience, and a faith that's pure gold. 🔥🔥

Love On Lock:

Love's the vibe, and it's gotta be on lock. Keep it 100 with the fam. Love deep, text back fast, and forgive like you're on a glitching Snapchat streak. It's all about that constant connection and community, no ghosting. 👻🖤

Humble Flex:

Stay humble, but let that goodness flex. It's not about clout; it's about that quiet grind of grace. Be the low-key MVP who's all about others. Let your actions drop those mics without needing to make a sound. 🎤🙏

Mind Over Matter:

Keep that mind tight and right. Be alert like you're waiting for that "item shipped" notification. Sober thoughts, big dreams. The world's your stream, so broadcast positivity and hope. 💭💭

Tough Skin, Soft Heart:

Develop that tough skin, but keep the heart soft. Life's gonna try to cancel you, but you've got that divine protection. Let the hate slide off like you're Teflon-coated, but keep your heart open like it's got unlimited data. 🛡️❤️

Be That Example:

Be the example, not the warning. Live so loud in your actions that your life's like that song everyone's got on repeat. Show 'em how it's done with kindness, respect, and a dash of holy swagger. 🎶🚶

Ride Out The Suffer:

When the suffering hits, ride it out like it's a wave. Remember, even the toughest levels have an endpoint. Keep that faith joystick steady, and power through. The victory screen is closer than you think.

Stay Charged:

Keep that spiritual battery charged. Prayer is your power bank, so stay connected to the Source. Keep those heavenly convos going like you're texting your crush.

End Game:

And remember, this ain't the end game. We're just in early levels. The final boss? Already defeated. The prize? It's eternal, and no one can snatch your trophy. So keep grinding, keep shining, and level up in that faith.

That's the 1 Peter Pep Talk, fam. Now go out there and be the vibe check the world needs. It's your time to glow up and show up, being all kinds of blessed and a blessing.

#1PeterPepTalk   #AncientWisdom   #GenZSlang #SpiritualHype #KeepTheFaith 🔥🚀🙌

The 2 Peter Warning Label 🔺🔥

Yo, Gen Z fam, let's get real and unpack this divine caution tape from the sequel, 2 Peter. It's the ancient tea, spilled for y'all, with a warning label that pops more than your fave influencer's latest viral vid. Strap in 'cause it's about to get 100% real. 💯

Beware of the Fakes:

First up, watch for the clout chasers and the truth twisters. These peeps are sliding into your DMs with fake news about the faith, trying to sell you a knockoff gospel that's more bootleg than a shady street vendor's merch. 🚫👥

Don't Trip on False Hype:

Don't get it twisted by those who flex a flashy lifestyle that's all smoke and no fire. They're all about that quick hype, but they're leading peeps down a glitchy path with no GPS. Stay woke, and keep your maps app pointed to The Truth. 🍎⚫

Real Recognize Real:

Real talk, the OG Apostle is telling you to keep your squad tight with genuine souls. If their lifestyle doesn't match their stories, they might just be catfishing your spirit. Swipe left on that mess. 💔⚫

Greed Ain't Good:

Watch out for those who treat faith like it's a cash grab game, turning blessings into a subscription service. Their hearts are like in-app purchases—always asking for more but never fulfilling. Keep your wallet and your soul on lockdown from these in-game scammers. 🌑 🔒

History's Lessons:

Remember the throwback episodes of humanity's fails, like heaven's own reality TV reruns. Those tales are there to school you on what not to do. Binge-watch those ancient lessons to avoid the same epic fails. 🪨 📺

No Co-Signing:

Don't co-sign on their lifestyle or their bad takes. When you see that red flag waving, don't try to paint it white. Keep your distance and don't endorse the mess. It's like clicking "agree" on the terms and conditions without reading—risky business. 🚩❌

Stay Alert:

Stay alert, fam. These false prophets and teachers are sneakier than a last-minute exam pop-up. They throw shade on the truth and try to remix it like a bad DJ. Keep your truth headphones on and don't let them mess with your playlist. 🎧👿

The Final Drop:

Here's the final drop—judgment's coming like the ultimate release date, and no one can avoid it. These posers will have to face the music, and it won't be their TikTok hit—it'll be the OG theme song of divine justice. ⌛🎶

Conclusion 🐛🔒

That's the 2 Peter Warning Label, peeps. Keep it locked on what's real, stay humble, and don't fall for the spiritual scam artists. Stick with the authentic, keep your faith verified, and your soul's account secure. It's a wild web out there, but you've got the divine antivirus—just make sure you keep it updated.

#2PeterWarning   #StayWoke   #FaithCheck #TruthOverTrends #GenZSlang 🔺👍📱

The 3 John Health Check 🔋✨

Ayo, Gen Z peeps! It's time to slide into the wellness zone with a quick health check, courtesy of the homie 3 John. This ancient script's got more life hacks than your fave wellness guru, and it's about to drop some holistic truth bombs for the soul and the 'gram. Let's get that spiritual and physical glow-up! 💪✨

Soul Fitness:

First things first, how's that soul feeling? Are you keeping it fit with daily reps of kindness, swiping right on good vibes, and eating clean with pure thoughts? Your inner health is key—gotta keep that spirit swole. 🏋️❤️

Truth Nutrition:

You are what you eat, right? Same goes for your mind. You been feeding it with that organic truth or you snackin' on some processed fake news? Keep your mental diet rich with the good stuff—straight from the source, no additives. 🍎📖

Love Cardio:

Get that heart rate up with some love cardio. Sprint towards those good deeds, jog past the drama, and keep the blood pumpin' with genuine connections. Remember, a heart workout is a daily thing. No rest days when it comes to love. 🖤🏃

Faith Hydration:

Hydrate, hydrate, hydrate! But we ain't just talkin' H2O—get that faith fluid in ya. It's the living water that keeps you refreshed and ready to face the desert of the daily grind. Keep sippin' on that spiritual spring. 💧🙏

Positivity Physio:

Sometimes the vibe gets injured from all the negativity, and you gotta hit up that positivity physio. Stretch out the kinks with some good news, strengthen those hope muscles, and rehab that outlook to full optimism. 🧘●

Community Checkups:

Don't skip those community checkups. Link with your peeps, share some encouragement, and check in on each other's progress. Healing happens in groups, so don't solo your way through the season. 🧚🧚🫂

Rest & Recovery:

You pushin' for that 24/7 hustle? Nah, fam. Even the Creator took a day off. Get that rest and recovery in. Power down the devices, meditate on the Word, and let your body and soul catch those Z's. 😴🛏

Eternal Insurance:

And don't forget to keep that eternal insurance policy active. Stay connected with the Big Boss, 'cause that's the coverage that comes with peace of mind and a no-worry policy. It's got you covered for all the afterlife gains. 📜🔒

Conclusion 🔚💯

That's the 3 John Health Check for ya. Keep thriving in truth, love like a boss, and maintain that balance—it's all about that holistic hustle. Stay spiritually jacked, mentally snatched, and heart-healthy, 'cause your best life is waiting both here and in the cloud.

#3JohnHealthCheck #SoulSwole #WellnessGlowUp #GenZSlang #HolisticHustle 📓✨🚀

Jude's Throwback 🔖

Yo, fam! Jude's got that old-school throwback story for all the Gen Z out there, and it's a vintage vibe check from way back. We're about to rewind and review this ancient message, so hit pause on that TikTok scroll and let's dive into the divine archives. 🎶⚫

Keepin' It Faithful:

Jude's kickin' it off with a shoutout to stay locked into that faith playlist, the one with the timeless bops. You gotta guard that belief like it's a limited-edition sneaker drop. Don't let anyone scuff your soul's J's. 🎧👟

Fake Fans Exposed:

There's some fake fans in the crowd, lowkey trying to sneak into the VIP section of your spiritual concert. These peeps are all about that backstage pass life, but they ain't got the real ticket—authentic love and devotion. 🚫🎟️

Throwback Warnings:

Jude's throwin' it back to the ultimate cautionary tales, highlighting the OG rebels who thought they could ghost God's DMs. Spoiler alert: it didn't end well. So keep your notifications on for that heavenly guidance. 💡➡️📱

Dreamer Disasters:

Watch out for them dreamers who got their heads in the cloud, but it's the wrong type of cloud—not the silver-lined ones. They're dreaming up ways to finesse the spiritual system, but trust, they're just playing themselves. 🌩️🎩

Divine Dealings:

Jude's reminding us that the Big Boss upstairs has had to deal with some serious rule-breakers before. And He's got that celestial justice on tap, ready to serve up to anyone trying to compromise the faith fam. ⚖️☝️

Archangel Attitude:

Even the archangel wasn't trying to flex in a face-off with the devil. He kept it classy, no trash talk, just left it to God to call the shots. That's a divine lesson in keeping your cool and letting karma do its thing.

Memorable Miracles:

Remember those epic miracle moments, the divine highlights that had everyone talking? Jude's saying don't forget those 'cause they're receipts of the real power and promises. They're the verified checkmarks in the history books.

Scoffers Gonna Scoff:

There's always gonna be trolls and scoffers, trying to clap back at your beliefs with their own weak tea. They're all about stirring the pot and causing division. Keep scrolling past that drama, no need to double-tap.

Build, Pray, Keep:

Jude's blueprint is simple: Build yourself up in the holy faith, get your prayer game strong, and keep yourself in the love zone with God. That's the spiritual gym routine for those gains that matter. 🏗️🙏❤️

Mercy Moves:

And when it comes to those struggling or tripping up, be about those mercy moves. Snatch them back from the edge with compassion and care. It's like being a spiritual lifeguard on duty. 🛟🤝

Conclusion 🌟💫

Jude's Throwback is a timeless call to keep it tight with faith, dodge those spiritual scams, and remember the OGs who set the stage. Stay true to the real ones, keep your heart tuned to that divine frequency, and show love like it's going out of style (it ain't, btw). That's how you keep your soul's story on the bestseller list.

#JudesThrowback   #FaithfulVibes   #GenZSlang #AncientWisdom #StayLit 🔥📕🛡️

The Revelation Reveal 🟫🍋

Ey, Gen Z squad! Strap in 'cause we're about to decode the ultimate spoiler alert, The Revelation Reveal. This ain't your everyday storytime; it's the final season teaser from the celestial series, and it's serving more drama than a reality TV finale. Get ready for a cosmic mind-blow!

Epic Intro:

John's kicking off this vision with a cinematic intro that's more extra than influencers at Coachella. He's getting downloads straight from the divine, and these aren't your standard 1080p dreams—it's full-on IMAX in the brain. 💭🎥

Seven Stars Flex:

First up, we've got the seven stars lineup, which is basically the heavenly version of the Avengers. They're the management team for the seven churches, keeping the holy hustle strong. ⭐

Letters to the Leaders:

These seven churches are getting the ultimate performance review via snail mail from the skies. Some are killing it, some need to step it up, and others are just a hot mess. It's like spiritual Yelp reviews straight from the throne. 👑

Seals, Trumpets, and Bowls – Oh My!:

Seals are getting broken, trumpets are blasting, and bowls are pouring out all sorts of wild stuff. It's a supernatural showcase of what happens when the universe starts dropping the bass. Each sound and sight is a sign that change is coming, and it's changing HARD. 🎺🏆

Beasts and Baddies:

We've got beasts popping up with more heads and horns than a monster truck rally. They're strutting around, trying to throw shade on the light, but they're just part of the show—plot twists in the grand scheme. 🐉👾

Number of the Game:

Keep an eye out for that infamous digit, 666—the number of the game. It's like the worst high score ever, and you don't wanna be on that leaderboard. Stay away from that cosmic malware. 🚫🟥

Heavenly Host Throwdown:

The ultimate throwdown is going down. It's angels versus the bad guys in a celestial smackdown that's more hyped than the Super Bowl. Spoiler: the angels don't need a halftime show to bring down the house. 😇🥊

New Heaven, New Earth:

After all the drama, we're hitting the reset button. A new heaven and a new Earth, where everything's HD crystal clear, and pain and tears are like those cringe trends from 2020—gone and forgotten. 🌐💧

VIP Access:

The grand finale is all about that VIP access to the divine city. We're talking streets of gold, gates of pearl, and a vibe so pure it's like the ultimate influencer paradise. No filters needed. ✨🟫

Eternal Lit-ness:

And the best part? The light never goes out. God's the eternal flame, keeping things lit forever—no energy-saving mode, just infinite brightness. It's the wrap party that never stops. 💡🎉

Conclusion 🚀❤️

The Revelation Reveal is a wild ride from start to finish, packed with more metaphors and symbols than a poet's group chat. It's a heads-up for the ultimate glow-up, so stay woke, keep your spirit game strong, and your heart tuned to the divine. This is the future, fam, and it's looking bright.

#RevelationReveal #CelestialSpoiler #GenZSlang #ApocalypseAesthetic #StayWokeEndTimes 🗣️🔥📖

The Seven Churches' DMs 📱⬛

Yo, Gen Z fam, let's spill the celestial tea 'cause John's out here sliding into the DMs of the seven churches with some heavenly hot takes. Get ready for a divine read receipt 'cause these messages are straight fire from the Big Boss's desk. #BlessedBeTheRead 🕊️🔥

Ephesus: The Hard-Working Hustlers 💼🚫❤️

@EphesusFam: Big ups for your no-quit game and fake-friend filters. But bro, where'd that first love vibe go? 💔 Don't ghost your heart, fam. Repent and hit that first-love refresh, or you'll be swiping left on your lampstand's light. #FirstLoveGlowUp

```
```

Smyrna: The No-Cap Sufferers 🫙 🎖️

@SmyrnaCrew: Peep this, you're in for a rough patch, no cap. But yo, stay 10 toes down. You might be broke AF, but you're rich in spirit. Crown emoji's waiting, just keep it 💯 through the pain. #SpiritualMillionaires

```


**Pergamum: The Complicated Crew** 🗡️ 👀

@PergamumPosse: Mad respect for holding it down where Satan's got his throne and all. But low-key, y'all got some in your squad that are vibin' with Balaam's old-school snafu. Time for a loyalty check, or I'mma pull up with a sharp two-edged sword. #KeepItRealOrKeepItMoving
```

```

## Thyatira: The Tolerant Ones 🏴‍☠️🚩

@ThyatiraTribe: Loving your work ethic and progress, fam. But we gotta talk about y'all letting Jezebel run wild with her VIP bad influence badge. Time to cancel that subscription. Stay true, or it's game over. #CancelCultureForJezebel

```

Sardis: The Reputation Rich 💤

@SardisSquad: Your rep's lit, but you're napping on the job. Wake up, fam! Tighten up before your spiritual fit check, or I'mma come through like a thief in the night. #WakeUpCall

```
```

Philadelphia: The Open-Door Gang 🔑

@PhillyFam: You kept it real with little power, and that's what's up. Hold tight to what you got, and no one can snatch your winner's wreath. I've set an open door in front of you, and ain't nobody closing that. #HoldFast #OpenDoorPolicy

```

## Laodicea: The Lukewarm Squad 🌡

@LaodiceaLads: So, we gotta address this lukewarm situation. You're neither icy nor steaming, and that's a whole vibe kill. You think you're Gucci, but you're actually thrift-store. Cop some gold refined in fire from me, and let's turn that heat up. #HotOrColdButNotLukewarm
```

```

## Conclusion 📖💯

These DMs from John are your personal notifications to keep your faith Wi-Fi strong and avoid spiritual dead zones. Whether you gotta step up your first-love game, keep your hustle holy, or just stop being so lukewarm, it's time to refresh your soul's signal. Stay blessed and double-tap on the divine.

#SevenChurchesDMs     #HeavenlyHotTakes

#FaithCheck #GenZSlang #DivineDMs 🙏📕♥
```

The Heavenly Worship Sesh 🎶🙌

Yo, celestial fam! Buckle up 'cause we're diving into the most epic worship sesh that's got the whole heaven popping off. It's like Coachella for your soul but way holier and with angels instead of influencers. Get ready to glow up in the worship game. #HeavenlyHype 🌟✨

The Throne Room Flex 🪑✨

Imagine the sickest VIP lounge, but holy. God's sitting on the throne, dripping in gemstone bling, and the whole place is shining brighter than your fave highlighter. Surround sound? Nah, we got living creatures with eyes all over—talk about a 360° view! #EyesEverywhere #ThroneRoomVibes

```

**Elders Rocking Crowns** 👑 ●

24 elders are chilling around the throne, decked out in white with crowns so icy they could freeze your screen. When the beat drops, they're throwing their crowns down like it's the hottest dance challenge. #CrownChallenge #ElderTikTok

```

Four Creatures, One Hype Squad 🐂 ● 🦅 ●

Four living creatures are straight-up out of a fantasy flick, each one repping a different vibe: lion, ox, human, and eagle. They've got one job: hyping up God 24/7 with a chant that's catchier than the latest bop. "Holy, holy, holy," on repeat, no remix needed. #HolyHolyHoly #NonStopWorship

```

**The Ultimate Sing-Along** 🎤 🔥

The creatures drop the chorus, and the elders come through with the verse. They're all about that worship life, singing their hearts out to the One who's been OG since before WiFi was a thing. It's like the whole room's on karaoke, but the lyrics are deep AF. #WorshipKaraoke #OGGod

```

Angelic Flash Mob 😇 🕺

Imagine a flash mob, but with angels. We're talking millions, and when they show up, it's straight-up breathtaking. They're in sync like they've got that divine Bluetooth connection, harmonizing about God's glory and power. #AngelicFlashMob #HeavenlyHarmony

```

### Universe-Wide Worship Wave 📱🙏

The whole scene's contagious. It starts with the throne room, but then it ripples out like the dopest TikTok challenge ever. Every creature in the universe is catching the wave, throwing in their own "Amen!" and "Praise!" It's a cosmic worship wave, and nobody's left out. #WorshipWave #CosmicPraise

```

Conclusion 📔

This heavenly worship sesh is next-level spiritual goals. It's where every tribe, tongue, and nation comes together for the ultimate throwdown in honor of the Big G. So wherever you're at, crank up your praise playlist and add some of that divine energy to your day. 'Cause when heaven throws a party, it's always lit. 🙌🎉

#HeavenlyWorshipSesh   #SpiritualGoals
#LitForTheLord #GenZWorship 🌟🙌💫

The Dragon and the Comeback Kid

🐉 ⚫

Yo, Gen Z squad! Buckle up 'cause we're diving into the ultimate showdown story. This tea's hotter than your fave influencer's scandal. We've got a dragon on one side and the ultimate Comeback Kid on the other. It's like a season finale that's got everyone on edge. #EpicShowdown 🎬🔥

The Dragon's Drama 🐉💥

First up, meet the dragon, Big Red. This dude's got clout like you wouldn't believe—seven heads, ten horns, and a mean streak that could ghost your good vibes. He's out here, tryna throw shade and chaos like

it's his day job. #BigBadRed #SevenHeadedHypeBeast
```

#### The Woman and the VIP Delivery 🤰✨

So, there's this woman decked out with the sun, moon, and a crown of twelve stars—talk about cosmic drip! She's 'bout to drop the most VIP baby of all time. Yeah, we're talking about the Comeback Kid. #CelestialMaternity #StarCrown
```

The Ultimate Birth and Snatch Attempt 👶👀

The baby arrives, destined to run the show. But here's the twist—Big Red's lurking, ready to snatch him up

the second he lands. It's like the worst kind of baby snatching, but cosmic edition. #NotTodaySatan #CelestialChildProtect
```

#### The Comeback Kid's Quick Exit 🚀🪨

But hold up, heaven's got a game plan. The Comeback Kid doesn't get snatched; he's zoomed up to the throne, VIP style. That's one small step for baby, one giant leap away from dragon drama. #HeavenlyEscape #ThroneBound
```

The Woman's Wilderness Glow-Up 🏜️👑

Meanwhile, the woman gets her own wilderness reality show, complete with divine protection. It's like "Survivor," but the angels are her production crew. #WildernessGlowUp #ProtectedByAngels

```

#### The Throwdown: Michael vs. Big Red 👼😈

Cue the ultimate celestial UFC: Archangel Michael and his angel crew throw hands with Big Red and his shady squad. It's a throwdown of biblical proportions, and spoiler alert: the dragon gets the boot. #CelestialUFC #MichaelVsDragon

```

The Dragon's Earthly Tantrum 🔴💥

Big Red's salty 'bout the L and starts throwing a tantrum on Earth. It's like a bad breakup, but with

fire and brimstone. #SoreLoserDragon #EarthlyChaos
```

#### The Comeback Kid's Future World Tour 🎤👑

Don't fret, 'cause the Comeback Kid's got a future comeback tour planned. When he hits the stage again, it's gonna be the biggest glow-up the world's ever seen. #ComebackTour #FutureKing
```

Conclusion 🏁🎤

The Dragon and the Comeback Kid is the story of the underdog flying high and the villain falling hard. It's got more twists than your favorite thriller and a happy ending still in the works. So, stay tuned, 'cause this saga's got sequels for days. Keep your eyes to the skies for the ultimate comeback.

#DragonDrama #ComebackKid #HeavenlyShowdown #GenZProphecy 📱👀💬

The Beast Mode Fail 🐾🚫

Yo, what's good, Gen Z crew? Strap in, 'cause I'm 'bout to spill the tea on the biggest "Beast Mode Fail" of the century. It's like watching someone flex for the 'Gram and then totally wipe out—except this time, it's apocalyptic. #EpicFail #BeastBusted 👤🔥

The Beast's Hype Game 🎤💪

Here's the sitch: there's this Beast, and dude's trying to build a rep like he's the next big influencer. He's got heads and horns and all that scary aesthetic, talking big game about power and authority. Think flexing in beast mode, but make it end-times. #BeastFlex #ApocaLit

```
```

The Worldwide Beast Fandom ●●●

This Beast's got followers, no cap. People are throwing likes and loyalty like he's dropping the hottest merch collab. It's a global fan club for this wannabe king of the jungle, all caught up in that beastly charisma. #WorldwideFandom #HornsUp

```

#### The Counterfeit Miracle Mix-Up 👀✨

Beast's pulling stunts, pretending to do the miraculous. It's like special effects IRL, trying to trick the masses into thinking he's got that divine connection. But it's all smoke and mirrors, fam. #FakeMiracles #SmokeAndMirrors

```

The Image That Wouldn't Stick ■●

Next thing, this Beast's crew sets up an image to make their boy look all-powerful. They're hyping it up like it's gonna go viral, but there's a catch—it's just a statue. No swipe-up feature, no live story, just stone-cold silence. #StatueSoNotLit #ImageFail

```

#### The Mark Miss Step 💔●

The Beast starts a trend, the "Mark." It's like a VIP pass to buying and selling, but the T&C's are sketchy as heck. It's an epic fail in the making 'cause it's more curse than perk. #MarkedForDisaster #WorstTrendEver

```

The Seven Bowls of Nope 🚫🍲

Just when the Beast thinks he's the it-creature, heaven's like, "Hold my chalice." Seven bowls of straight-up nope are poured out, and suddenly, Beast Mode's looking real glitchy. It's like cosmic karma, and it's got his number. #SevenBowlsOfNope #HeavenClapsBack

```

#### The Final Boss Battle Flop 🎮⚫

Roll up to the final boss battle, and it's the Beast and his posse versus the Big JC and the cavalry of heaven. Spoiler alert: The Beast's mode ain't got nothing on the King of Kings. It's game over for the faux beast,
```

and he's not respawning. #BossBattleBust #GameOverBeast

```

### Conclusion 📕💔

The Beast Mode Fail is a lesson in what happens when you try to play god without the cheat codes. It's a total wipeout, a fall from clout, a crash from that high. So, let's leave beast mode to the video games and focus on keeping it real with the good vibes and the truth.

#BeastWipeout #StayHumble #RealRecognizeReal #GenZEndTimes 🤘⛈️👑
```

The Angels' Hot Takes 🔥😇

Yo, Gen Z fam! Get ready for the most fire takes straight from the angels themselves. We're not talking about your everyday tea; this is the divine gossip column, celestial edition. The angels are dishing out their thoughts and it's about to get lit. #HeavenlyHotTakes #AngelSpillTheTea 🍵✨

On Human Shenanigans 👀⚫

Angels be like, "Humans are wildin' out down there," watching us do the most with our drama and TikTok challenges. It's a mix of facepalms and heart emojis because they see us struggling but also catching

those small wins. #FacepalmMoments #HumanShenanigans
```

#### On #Blessed Vibes 🙌🖤

When we're out here counting our blessings and staying grateful, angels are totally here for it. They're hyping us up like a divine cheer squad, 'cause nothing slaps harder in heaven than a thankful heart. #StayBlessed #GratitudeGang
```

On Keeping It Real 🚫🖤

Angels keeping it 100, reminding us that authenticity is key. They've seen every trend come and go, and they know that realness lasts longer than any viral dance. So keep it genuine, and you'll be on that eternal glow-up. #AuthenticityWins #EternalGlowUp

```

#### On Environmental Care 🌿🌍

Heavenly hosts are all about that green life—no, not money, Earth! They're looking at us like, "Can y'all please recycle?" 'Cause they know Mother Nature isn't just a trend, it's the OG home. #EcoWarriors #PlanetProtectors

```

On Spiritual Wi-Fi 📶🙏

These celestial beings are low-key confused by how we ignore our spiritual Wi-Fi. We've got unlimited access to peace and love, but we're out here tryna connect to every other network. Angels are like, "Just hit up the divine hotspot, it's got full bars!" #SpiritualWiFi #DivineConnection

```

#### **On Being Extra** 😇

Angels are vibing with people who go the extra mile to be kind. It's like when someone helps a stranger or spreads positivity, angels are giving standing ovations. They're all about that extra sprinkle of love in a world that can be salty. #KindnessIsExtra #SpreadLove

```

On FOMO and JOMO 🚫🎉✨🏔️

Angels are watching us sweat over FOMO and they're like, "Chill, humans." They're the OG fans of JOMO 'cause they know the joy of missing out is underrated. Sometimes the holiest thing you can do is rest, and they're all for that self-care sabbatical. #JOMO #HeavenlySelfCare

```

#### On Celestial Tea

When it comes to spilling the tea, angels have the celestial brew on lock. They've seen it all from their high-key heavenly perspective, and they're sipping the good stuff, waiting for us to catch up to the eternal truths. #CelestialTea #HeavenlyPerspective

```

Conclusion 🎤✨

The angels' hot takes are all about love, truth, and keeping it real. They've got the best seats in the house and the wisest whispers in our ears. So let's vibe with those angelic insights and keep our spirits tuned to the divine frequencies. Stay blessed, stay woke, and remember, the angels got your back.

#AngelicWisdom #HeavenlyHotGoss
#GenZAngelTakes #HolyHotline ☁️📞💜

The Babylon Block ■🚫

Ayo, Gen Z squad! Time to decode the 411 on The Babylon Block. Picture the ultimate ghost town, but make it ancient and extra. Babylon's like that one influencer who tried to flex too hard and got shadowbanned by the universe. #ByeByeBabylon #EpicGhosting 🎤👻

The High-Key Hype Buildup 🏗️💥

Babylon was out here trying to build to the sky, no joke. They wanted that clout, to be the GOAT of cities with a tower touching the clouds—total skyscraper goals. But it was less about the sky and more about that ego life. #SkyHighEgo #TowerFail

```

#### **The Clout Chasers' Confusion** 🌑👥

So everyone's speaking the same language, right? Vibing and collaborating. Then, boom! The universe hits 'em with the biggest plot twist: the language barrier. It's like autocorrect gone wild, no one understands each other. #BabelBabble #LostInTranslation

```

The Divine Dislike 👎⚡

The cosmos was not having it with this Babylon flex. It's like the divine algorithm decided to shadowban the whole project. Suddenly, it's no longer trending,

and the unity playlist is on shuffle.
#DivineIntervention #CosmicUnfollow
```

#### **The Scatter Plot** 🌐 🏃

Post language mix-up, everyone's like, "We out." It's the original ghosting. People scatter faster than a Gen Z'er's attention span when the Wi-Fi drops. Babylon went from the place to be to nobody's home. #ScatterFest #BabylonBlockPartyOver
```

The Legacy That Didn't Last 🗿 👳

Babylon's trying to leave a legacy, but it ends up a cautionary tale. It's like posting a pic you think will break the internet, but it ends up being a reminder to stay humble or get dragged. #LegacyOrLesson #StayHumbleFam

```

#### The Moral of the Story ✨📖

The Babylon Block is that ancient tea that spills itself. It's telling us to check our motives and remember where we come from. Don't build towers of ego; build bridges of connection. #RealTalk #BuildBridgesNotTowers

```

Conclusion 📓🌟

So here's the lowdown: The Babylon Block shows that when we vibe for the wrong reasons, things can tumble down real quick. Let's keep our ambitions legit and our communities tight. Build with purpose, speak with clarity, and maybe, just maybe, we won't get blocked by the big algorithm in the sky.

#BabylonLesson   #HumbleVibes   #GenZHistory #AncientTeaSpilled 🌿🗿💡

The New 'Gram and the Real Influencer 📸✨

Yo, Gen Z peeps! Scope this: We're spillin' the deets on The New 'Gram and the one who's actually got the juice to be called the Real Influencer. Forget the basic feed aesthetics; we're talkin' 'bout an influencer who's not just about that #SponCon life. #AuthenticVibesOnly #RealInfluencer 🌟

The New 'Gram Glow-Up 🌐🔥

The 'Gram's got a facelift, y'all. It ain't just about those Valencia-filtered brunch pics anymore. We're here for the raw, the real, the stories that hit different. It's a platform glow-up where authenticity isn't just a hashtag, it's the whole vibe. #NewGramGlowUp #NoFilterNeeded

```

#### The Clout Game Change 🎮⬛

Forget the follow-for-follow, the bots, and the bought likes. The clout game's switching up. Real Influencer's not about chasing metrics but making an impact. They're the trendsetter with a cause, the voice for the voiceless. #CloutWithACause #GameChanger

```

The Hashtag Hero 🏷️🏷️

This influencer? They're hashtag goals, fam. They're out here starting movements, not just trends. They're the hashtag hero we didn't know we needed, turning double taps into acts of kindness and awareness. #HashtagHero #MoreThanALike

```

#### The Swipe-Up Revolution 📱✊

When Real Influencer drops a "Swipe Up," it ain't for detox teas or flash sales. It's for petitions, charities, and community drives. They're using that swipe-up power to uplift, not just upsell. #SwipeUpRevolution #SwipeForGood

```

The DMs of Destiny 📩🌟

DMs are slidin' in with purpose now. Real Influencer's inbox is about connection, support, and empowerment. They're the real deal, chatting with followers about more than just the latest drop. #DMsofDestiny #RealTalk

```

####### The New 'Gram and the Real Influencer 📺✨

#### Yo, Gen Z fam! Peep the scene on The New 'Gram and the OG influencer who's servin' up more than just looks. We're talkin' 'bout the one who's out here shaping the culture, slayin' the game with authenticity, and throwin' major shade at the fake. #KeepinItReal #InfluenceWithPurpose 🚀

#### The 'Gram's Fresh Face 📱👀
```

The 'Gram's been rebooted, and it's all about that genuine content now, no cap. It's the digital renaissance of real talk, where filters take a backseat to stories that slap. This platform's not just a stage; it's a megaphone for the woke and the wise. #NewGramNewMe #RealOverReels

```

#### The Clout Culture Shift 📱💯

The clout chase is overrated, and our Real Influencer knows it. They're flippin' the script, ditchin' the superficial for something substantial. It's not about the likes; it's about the impact, the kind that resonates IRL. #BeyondTheLikes #CloutWithConscience

```

The Vibe Check Virtuoso 📱👉

This influencer's vibe check is a whole mood. They're the virtuoso of good vibes, spreading positivity like it's confetti at a parade. They make scrolling through your feed feel like a breath of fresh air. #VibeCheckPassed #GoodVibesOnly

```

#### The Storyteller Supreme 📖👑

They're not just posting; they're storytelling with a purpose. Every pic, every caption, every story they share is a chapter in a larger narrative about what's real and what matters. #StorytellingSupreme #CaptionsThatCount

```

The Engagement Enthusiast 💬 ♥

Engagement isn't just a metric; it's a mission. The Real Influencer's replies and DMs are where support systems are built and voices get amplified. They're the proof that behind every username is a heart and a story. #EngagementEnthusiast #HeartfeltDMs

```

#### The Movement Maker 🏃 ●

When this influencer says "Link in bio," it's not a trap; it's a trampoline to higher ground. They're the launchpad for movements that matter, from sustainability to social justice. They're not just in your feed; they're leading the charge for change. #MovementMaker #LinkInBioForChange
```

```

### Conclusion 🎤🔥

The New 'Gram and the Real Influencer are the antidote to the basic. They're the heart in the algorithm, the soul behind the screen. They remind us that influence isn't about the flex; it's about the footprint you leave on the world. So let's double-tap that reality and make every post a step towards something epic.

#GenZInfluence          #RealnessRevolution
#ChangeTheFeed #InfluencersThatInspire 🌟🌙🌿
```

TL; DR (TOO LONG; DIDN'T READ)📖📕

JC's Birth - #StableBday 👶✨

Virgin Mary's like, "OMG, angel says I'm preggers with God's kiddo!" Joseph's chill with it. Jesus drops in a manger; wise dudes bring gifts. Major birthday flex.

```

#### Water to Wine - #PartySavior 🍷🎉

Jesus at a wedding, they out of Merlot. He's like, "BRB," turns H2O into the best vino. First miracle and the guests are living for it.

```

Squad Goals - #DiscipleSquad 🎣👥

Jesus is like, "Yo, fishers of fish, let's be fishers of peeps." Disciples yeet their nets, follow the vibe. Apostles assemble!

```

#### Sermon on the Mount - #BlessedBeats 🏔️🙏

Jesus hits the hill, spits pure fire blessings, talks peace, love, and being salt of the Earth. Crowd's mind = blown.

```

Loaves & Fishes - #HolyMukbang 🍞🐟

5K hungry homies, Jesus has 5 bread, 2 fish. Blesses it, breaks it, feeds all. Leftovers for days. How? Divine DoorDash.

```

#### Walk on Water - #H2Whoa 👣💧
```

Disciples in a boat, see Jesus strolling on waves like it's NBD. Peter tries, sinks, Jesus saves. Faith level: Titanic.

```

#### Good Samaritan - #NeighborGoals 🫂🖤

Guy gets jumped, left for dead. Peeps pass by, do nada. Samaritan dude's like, "I gotchu," help him. That's the tea on being neighborly.

```

Prodigal Son - #ComebackKid 🏠💰

Dude blows his cash, hits rock bottom, crawls home. Dad throws a massive welcome back bash. It's all about that forgiveness flex.

```

#### Lazarus - #DeathWho 🪦⬛
```

Jesus's bud Lazarus dies, Jesus rolls up 4 days late, like, "Laz, wakey-wakey," and dude's like, "Zombie life, but make it holy."

```

#### Last Supper - #OGCommunion 🍞🍷

Jesus and the crew have one last dinner, Jesus is like, "Eat this bread, it's me; drink this wine, it's my blood." Disciples: "That's deep."

```

Judas Betrayal - #NotCoolBro 💔🐍

Judas kisses Jesus, not in a bro way, but a "you're gonna get arrested" way. 30 silver coins, and he's out. Et tu, Brute?

```

#### Crucifixion - #UltimateSacrifice ⬛⚫
```

Jesus gets the cross, it's brutal, but he's doing it for humanity. "It's finished," then it lights out for our savior.

```

#### Resurrection - #HeIsRisen 🪦✨

Third day, Jesus is like, "Back at it," rolls the stone, beats death. Disciples hyped, Thomas doubts, then believes. Easter, anyone?

```

Pentecost - #HolyGhostParty 🔥🕊️

Disciples chilling, Holy Spirit crashes in like a wind, tongues of fire on heads. Everyone's speaking different languages, still vibin'.

```

#### Paul's Redemption - #BlindedByTheLight 🎥👀
```

Saul's hating on Christians, gets a holy light zap en route to Damascus. Now he's Paul, preaching Jesus-game strong.

```

#### Revelation - #SpoilerAlert 🐉 👁

John's trippy dream: 7 seals, 4 horsemen, some beasts, and mad judgments. Spoiler: God's team wins. Heaven's gates, open for the real ones.

```

The Wrap-Up 📕🙏

That's your New Testament crash course, Gen Z style. Jesus was out here doing the most, flipping scripts, and setting the bar for influencers everywhere. Stay blessed, fam. #AmenAndAmen 🕊️✨

GLOSSARY ✊✌

Apostles - #SquadGoals 🏀

The OG crew, Jesus' main 12. They're the ride-or-die peeps spreading the good news after Jesus ascended. Think of them as the divine influencers.

Bethlehem - #BirthplaceBanger 📍🏺

Tiny town where Jesus decided to make his grand entrance. Pretty much the OG viral event location.

Crucifixion - #CrossFitExtreme ⬛⚫

Not the workout kind. This is the intense part where Jesus got put on the cross. Major sacrifice vibes.

Disciples - #FollowerFam 👥

The broader squad beyond the main 12. Anyone down with Jesus' teachings and rolling deep with his message.

Gospel - #HolyContent 📕✨

The four books Matthew, Mark, Luke, and John spitting straight facts about Jesus' life. It's the biblical version of a vlog series.

Judas - #BetrayalBuddy 🎭🐍

The dude who traded his loyalty to Jesus for some silver. Showed that not all kisses are friendly.

Last Supper - #FinalFeast 🍞🍷

Jesus' last meal with the squad where he dropped some serious truth bombs about betrayal and sacrifice. Also, bread and wine got a whole new meaning.

Messiah - #SaviorSupreme ✨👑

The one everyone's been waiting for. Jesus is the main man with the plan for humanity's redemption.

Miracles - #FlexingTheDivine 💪✨

When Jesus went full beast mode with the supernatural acts. Water into wine, feeding thousands, healing the sick—big power moves.

Parables - #StorytimeWithJ 💬💡

Jesus' way of dropping knowledge through stories. Think of them as life hacks but make them spiritual.

Pharisees - #RulePolice 👤🚓

The religious high-key haters of Jesus. They loved the law more than the vibe of love and mercy Jesus was preaching.

Resurrection - #ComebackKing 🪦👑

Jesus said "BRB" after death and actually came back. The ultimate "you thought" moment.

Revelation - #SpoilerAlertEndGame 🎙️🏆

The final book where John spills the tea on how everything will go down at the very end. Dragons, angels, and some serious CGI-worthy action.

Salvation - #EternalLifeHack ✨🎬

The whole point of the game. Jesus offered a way to beat death and sin, kind of like the ultimate cheat code for life.

Sin - #OopsCulture ⚫🚫

All the bad stuff we do that separates us from God. Jesus is like the ultimate antivirus for this mess.

Trinity - #DivineTrio 🕊️✨

The Father, Son, and Holy Spirit. It's like a divine squad in one, the ultimate team-up.

Virgin Mary - #MiracleMom 🙏👶

Jesus' mom who had the most epic "I'm pregnant" story ever. Literally gave birth to the biggest plot twist in human history.

Wrap It Up 🎁🔥

And that's the down-low on the New Testament terms, Gen Z style. Keep it fresh, keep it 100, and keep those blessings on tap. #StayWokeToTheWord 📖✨

Printed in Great Britain
by Amazon